The Book of Tobit

Ancient Texts and Translations

Series Editor
K. C. Hanson

Robert William Rogers
Cuneiform Parallels to the
Old Testament

D. Winton Thomas, editor
Documents from
Old Testament Times

Henry Frederick Lutz
Early Babylonian Letters
from Larsa

Albert T. Clay
Babylonian Epics, Hymns,
Omens, and Other Texts

Daniel David Luckenbill
The Annals of Sennacherib

A. E. Cowley
Aramaic Papyri of the
Fifth Century B.C.

G. R. Driver
Aramaic Documents of the
Fifth Century B.C., rev. ed.

Adolf Neubauer
The Book of Tobit

August Dillman
The Ethiopic Text of 1 Enoch

R. H. Charles
The Apocrypha and
Pseudepigrapha of the
Old Testament

R. H. Charles
The Book of Enoch

R. H. Charles
The Book of Jubilees

R. H. Charles
The Testaments of the
Twelve Patriarchs

R. H. Charles
The Apocalypse of Baruch

H. B. Swete
The Gospel of Peter

Richard Adelbert Lipsius
and Max Bonnet
Apocryphal Acts
of the Apostles (3 vols.)

The Book of Tobit
The Text in Aramaic, Hebrew, and Old Latin with English Translations

Edited by
Adolf Neubauer

Wipf & Stock Publishers
Eugene, Oregon

THE BOOK OF TOBIT
The Text in Aramaic, Hebrew, and Old Latin with
English Translations Ancient Texts and Translations

ISBN: 1-59752-374-7

Manufactured in the U.S.A.

Contents

Series Foreword

The discoveries of documents from the ancient Near Eastern and Mediterranean worlds have altered our modern understanding of those worlds in both breadth and depth. Especially since the mid-nineteenth century, chance discoveries as well as archaeological excavations have brought to light thousands of clay tablets, stone inscriptions and stelae, leather scrolls, codices, papyri, seals, and ostraca.

The genres of these written documents are quite diverse: receipts, tax lists, inventories, letters, prophecies, blessings and curses, dowry documents, deeds, laws, instructions, collections of proverbs, philosophical treatises, state propaganda, myths and legends, hymns and prayers, liturgies and rituals, and many more. Some of them came to light in long-famous cities—such as Ur, Babylon, Nineveh, and Jerusalem—while others came from locations that were previously little-known or unknown— such as Ebla, Ugarit, Elephantine, Qumran, and Nag Hammadi.

But what good are these remnants from the distant past? Why should anyone bother with what are often fragmentary, ob-scure, or long-forgotten scraps of ancient cultures? Each person will answer those questions for herself or himself, depending upon interests and commitments. But the documents have influ-enced scholarly research in several areas.

It must first be said that the documents are of interest and importance in their own right, whatever their connections—or lack of them—to modern ethnic, religious, or ideological con-cerns. Many of them provide windows on how real people lived in the ancient world—what they grew and ate; how they related to their families, business associates, and states; how they were taxed; how and whom they worshiped; how they organized their communities; their hopes and fears; and how they understood and portrayed their own group's story.

They are of intense interest at the linguistic level. They pro-vide us with previously unknown or undeciphered languages and dialects, broaden our range of vocabularies and meanings, assist us in mapping the relationships and developments of languages, and provide examples of loan-words and linguistic influences between languages. A monumental project such as *The Assyrian Dictionary,* produced by the Oriental Institute at the University of Chicago, would have been unthinkable without the broad range of Akkadian resources today.[1] And our study of Coptic and early gospels would be impoverished without the Nag Hammadi codices.[2]

The variety of genres also attracts our interest in terms of the history of literature. Such stories as Athra-hasis, Enumma Elish, and Gilgamesh have become important to the study of world literature. While modern readers may be most intrigued by something with obvious political or religious content, we often learn a great deal from a tax receipt or a dowry document. Her-

---

[1] I. J. Gelb et al., editors, *The Assyrian Dictionary of the Oriental Institute of the University of Chicago* (Chicago: Univ. of Chicago Press, 1956–).

[2] James M. Robinson, editor, *The Nag Hammadi Library in English,* 3d ed. (San Francisco: HarperSanFrancisco, 1990).

mann Gunkel influenced biblical studies not only because of his keen insights into the biblical books, but because he studied the biblical genres in the light of ancient Near Eastern texts. As he examined the genres in the Psalms, for example, he compared them to the poetic passages throughout the rest of the Bible, the Apocrypha, the Pseudepigrapha, Akkadian sources, and Egyp-tian sources.[3] While the Akkadian and Egyptian resources were much more limited in the 1920s and 1930s when he was working on the Psalms, his methodology and insights have had an on-going significance.

History is also a significant interest. Many of these texts mention kingdoms, ethnic and tribal groups, rulers, diplomats, generals, locations, or events that assist in establishing chronol-ogies, give us different perspectives on previously known events, or fill in gaps in our knowledge. Historians can never have too many sources. The Amarna letters, for example, provide us with the names of local rulers in Canaan during the fourteenth century BCE, their relationship with the pharaoh, as well as the military issues of the period.[4]

Social analysis is another area of fertile research. A deed can reveal economic structures, production, land tenure, kinship rela-tions, scribal conventions, calendars, and social hierarchies. Both the Elephantine papyri from

---

[3] Hermann Gunkel, *Einleitung in die Psalmen: Die Gattungen der religiösen Lyrik Israels,* completed by Joachim Begrich, HAT (Göttingen: Vandenhoeck & Ruprecht, 1933). ET = *Introduction to the Psalms: The Genres of the Religious Lyric of Israel,* trans. James D. Nogalski, Mercer Library of Biblical Studies (Macon, Ga.: Mercer Univ. Press, 1998).

[4] William L. Moran, *The Amarna Letters* (Baltimore: Johns Hopkins Univ. Press, 1992).

Egypt (fifth century BCE) and the Babatha archive from the Judean desert (second century CE) include personal legal documents and letters relating to dowries, inheritance, and property transfers that provide glimpses of com-plex kinship relations, networking, and legal witnesses.[5] And the Elephantine documents also include letters to the high priest in Jerusalem from the priests of Elephantine regarding the rebuild-ing of the Elephantine temple.

Religion in the ancient world was usually embedded in either political or kinship structures. That is, it was normally a function of either the political group or kin-group to which one belonged. We are fortunate to have numerous texts of epic literature, liturgies, and rituals. These include such things as creation stories, purification rituals, and the interpretation of sheep livers for omens. The Dead Sea Scrolls, for example, provide us with biblical books, texts of biblical interpretation, community regula-tions, and liturgical texts from the second temple period.[6]

Another key element has been the study of law. A variety of legal principles, laws, and collections of regulations provide windows on social structures, economics, governance, property rights, and

---

[5] Bezalel Porten et al., editors, *The Elephantine Papyri in English: Three Millennia of Cross-Cultural Continuity and Change*, Documenta et Monumenta Orientis Antiqui 22 (Leiden: Brill, 1996); Yigael Yadin et al., *The Finds from the Bar Kokhba Period in the Cave of Letters*, 3 vols., Judean Desert Studies (Jerusalem: Israel Exploration Society, 1963–2002) [NB: vols. 2 and 3 are titled *Documents* instead of *Finds*].

[6] Florentino Garcia Martinez, *The Dead Sea Scrolls Translated: The Qumran Texts in English*, 2d ed., trans. Wilfred G. E. Watson (Grand Rapids: Eerdmans, 1996).

punishments. The stele of Hammurabi of Babylon (c. 1700 BCE) is certainly the most famous. But we have many more, for example: Ur-Nammu (c. 2100 BCE), Lipit-Ishtar (c. 1850 BCE), and the Middle Assyrian Laws (c. 1150 BCE).

The intention of Ancient Texts and Translations (ATT) is to make available a variety of ancient documents and document collections to a broad range of readers. The series will include reprints of long out-of-print volumes, revisions of earlier editions, and completely new volumes. The understanding of an-cient societies depends upon our close reading of the documents, however fragmentary, that have survived.

—K. C. Hanson
Series Editor

Select Bibliography

I. Editions and Translations

Fitzmyer, Joseph A. "Preliminary Publication of pap4QTob[a] ar, Fragment 2." *Biblica* 75 (1994) 220–24.

———. "The Aramaic and Hebrew Fragments of Tobit from Qumran Cave 4." *Catholic Biblical Quarterly* 57 (1995) 655–75.

———. *Tobit.* Commentaries on Early Jewish Literature. Berlin: de Gruyter, 2003.

Hanhart, Robert. *Text und Textgeschichte des Buches Tobit.* Mitteilungen des Septuaginta-Unternehmens 17. Göttingen: Vandenhoeck & Ruprecht, 1984.

James, Montague R. *The Book of Tobit and the History of Susanna.* London: Haymarket, 1929.

Moore, Carey A. *Tobit.* Anchor Bible 40A. New York: Doubleday, 1996.

Schneider, H., W. Baars, and J. C. H. Lebram, editors. *Canticles or Odes; Prayer of Manasseh; Apocryphal Psalms; Psalms of Solomon; Tobit; 1 (3) Esdras.* The Old Testament in Syriac, according to the Peshitta Version 4/6. Leiden: Brill, 1972.

Simpson, D. C. "Tobit." In *The Apocrypha and Pseudepigrapha of the Old Testament in English,* 2 vols., edited by R. H. Charles, 1:174–241. Oxford: Clarendon, 1913.

Skemp, Vincent T. M. *The Vulgate of Tobit Compared with Other Ancient Witnesses.* SBL Dissertation Series. Atlanta: Society of Biblical Literature, 2000.

Wills, Lawrence M., editor and translator. *Ancient Jewish Novels: An Anthology.* New York: Oxford University Press, 2002.

Zimmerman, Frank. *The Book of Tobit.* Jewish Apocryphal Literature. New York: Harper, 1958.

II. Research

Blenkinsopp, Joseph. "Biographical Patterns in Biblical Narrative." *Journal for the Study of the Old Testament* 20 (1981) 27–46.

Bow, Beverly, and George W. E. Nickelsburg. "Patriarchy with a Twist: Men and Women in Tobit." In *"Women Like This": New Perspectives on Jewish Women in the Greco-Roman World,* edited by Amy-Jill Levine, 127–43. Early Judaism and Its Literature 1. Atlanta: Scholars , 1991.

Cook, Edward M. "Our Translated Tobit." In *Targumic and Cognate Studies: Studies in Honour of Martin McNamara,* edited by Kevin J. Cathcart and Michael Maher, 153–62. Journal for the Study of the Old Testament Supplement Series 230. Sheffield: Sheffield Academic, 1996.

Cousland, J. R. C. "Tobit: A Comedy in Error?" *Catholic Biblical Quarterly* 65 (2003) 535–53.

Craghan, John. *Esther, Judith, Tobit, Jonah, Ruth.* Old Testament Message 16. Wilmington, Del.: Glazier, 1982.

Day, Linda. "Power, Otherness, and Gender in the Biblical Short Stories." *Horizons in Biblical Theology* 20 (1998) 109–27.

Deselaers, Paul. *Das Buch Tobit: Studien zu seiner Entstehung, Komposition und Theologie.* Orbis biblicus et orientalis 43. Göttingen: Vandenhoeck & Ruprecht, 1982.

Doran, Robert. "Narrative Literature." In *Early Judaism and Its Modern Interpreters,* edited by George W. E. Nickelsburg, 287–310. Philadelphia: Fortress, 1986.

Egger-Wenzel, Renate, and Jeremy Corley, editors. *Prayer from Tobit to Qumran: Inaugural Conference of the ISDCL at Salzburg, Austria, 5-9 July 2003.* Deuterocanonical and Cognate Literature Yearbook 2004. Berlin: de Gruyter, 2004.

Fitzmyer, Joseph A. "The Significance of the Hebrew and Aramaic Texts of Tobit from Qumran for the Study of Tobit." In *The Dead Sea Scrolls,* 418–25. Jerusalem: Israel Exploration Society, 2000.

———. *Tobit.* Commentaries on Early Jewish Literature. Berlin: de Gruyter, 2003.

Handy, Lowell K. *Entertaining Faith: Reading Short Stories in the Bible.* St. Louis: Chalice, 2000.

Levine, Amy-Jill. "Diaspora as Metaphor: Bodies and Boundaries in the Book of Tobit." In *Diaspora Jews and Judaism: Essays in Honor of, and in Dialogue with, A. Thomas Kraabel,* edited by J. Andrew Overman and Robert S. MacLennan, 105–17. South Florida Studies in the History of Judaism 41. Atlanta: Scholars, 1992.

———. "Tobit: Teaching Jews How to Live in the Diaspora." *Bible Review* 8.4 (1992) 42–51, 64.

MacDonald, Dennis R. Tobit and the Odyssey." In *Mimesis and Intertextuality in Antiquity and Christianity,* edited by Dennis R. MacDonald, 11–40. Studies in Antiquity and Christianity. Harrisburg, Pa.: Trinity, 2001.

McCracken, David. "Narration and Comedy in the Book of Tobit." *Journal of Biblical Literature* 114 (1995) 401–18.

Millard, Alan R. "Judith, Tobit, Ahiqar and History." In *New Heaven and New Earth—Prophecy and the Millennium: Essays in Honour of Anthony Gelston,* edited by P. J. Harland and C. T. R. Hayward, 195–203. Vetus Testamentum Supplements 77. Leiden: Brill, 1999.

Miller, James E. "The Redaction of Tobit and the Genesis Apocryphon." *Journal for the Study of the Pseudepigrapha* 8 (1991) 53–61.

Milne, Pamela J. "Folktales and Fairy Tales: An Evaluation of Two Proppian Analyses of Biblical Narratives." *Journal for the Study of the Old Testament* 34 (1986) 35–60.

Moore, Carey A. "Scholarly Issues in the Book of Tobit before Qumran and After: An Assessment." *Journal for the Study of the Pseudepigrapha* 5 (1989) 65–81.

———. *Tobit.* Anchor Bible 40A. New York: Doubleday, 1996.

Nickelsburg, George W. E. "Tobit and Enoch: Distant Cousins with a Recognizable Resemblance." *SBL Seminar Papers* 27 (1988) 54–68.

———. "The Search for Tobit's Mixed Ancestry: A Historical and Hermeneutical Odyssey." *Revue de Qumran* 17 (1996) 339–49.

———. "Tobit, Genesis, and the Odyssey: A Complex Web of Intertextuality." In *Mimesis and Intertextuality in Antiquity and Christianity,* edited by Dennis R. MacDonald, 41–55. Studies in Antiquity and Christianity. Harrisburg, Pa.: Trinity, 2001.

Nowell, Irene. "The Narrator in the Book of Tobit." *SBL Seminar Papers* 27 (1988) 27–38.

Otzen, Benedikt. *Tobit and Judith.* Guides to Apocrypha and Pseudepigrapha Series. London: Sheffield Academic, 2002.

Portier-Young, Anathea. "Alleviation of Suffering in the Book of Tobit: Comedy, Community, and Happy Endings." *Catholic Biblical Quarterly* 63 (2001) 35–54.

Rabenau, Merten. *Studien zum Buch Tobit.* Beihefte zur Zeitschrift für die alttestamentliche Wissenschaft 220. Berlin: de Gruyter, 1994.

Skemp, Vincent. "*Adelphos* and the Theme of Kinship in Tobit." *Ephemerides theologicae Lovanienses* 75 (1999) 92–103.

Soll, Will. "Tobit and Folklore Studies, with Emphasis on Propp's Morphology." *SBL Seminar Papers* 27 (1988) 39–53.

———. "Misfortune and Exile in Tobit: The Juncture of a Fairy Tale Source and Deuteronomic Theology." *Catholic Biblical Quarterly* 51 (1989) 209–31.

———. "The Family as Scriptural and Social Construct in Tobit." In *The Function of Scripture in Early Jewish and Christian Tradition,* edited by Craig A. Evans and James A. Sanders, 166–75. Journal for the Study of the New Testament 154. Sheffield: Sheffield Academic, 1998.

Spencer, Richard A. "The Book of Tobit in Recent Research." *Currents in Research: Biblical Studies* 7 (1999) 147–80.

Weitzman, Steven. "Allusion, Artifice, and Exile in the Hymn of Tobit." *Journal of Biblical Literature* 115 (1996) 49–61.

Wills, Lawrence M. *The Jewish Novel in the Ancient World*. Myth and Poetics. Ithaca, N.Y.: Cornell Univ. Press, 1995.

———. "The Depiction of Slavery in the Ancient Novel." *Semeia* 83/84 (1998) 113–32.

Xeravits, Géza G., and József Zsengellér, editors. *The Book of Tobit: Text, Tradition, Theology. Papers of the First International Conference on the Deuterocanonical Books, Pápa, Hungary, 20-21 May, 2004.* Leiden: Brill, 2005.

PREFACE.

JEROME, in his preface to the translation of Tobit, says that he translated it from a Chaldee text. We give his own words[1]:

'Chromatio et Heliodoro Episcopis Hieronymus Presbyter in Domino salutem.

'Mirari non desino exactionis vestrae instantiam: exigitis enim, ut librum Chaldaeo sermone conscriptum ad Latinum stylum traham, librum utique Tobiae, quem Hebraei de catalogo divinarum Scripturarum secantes, his, quae Apocrypha memorant, manciparunt. Feci satis desiderio vestro, non tamen meo studio. Arguunt enim nos Hebraeorum studia, et imputant nobis contra suum canonem Latinis auribus ista transferre. Sed melius esse judicans Pharisaeorum displicere judicio, et Episcoporum jussionibus deservire, institi ut potui. Et quia vicina est Chaldaeorum lingua sermoni Hebraico, utriusque linguae peritissimum loquacem reperiens, unius diei laborem arripui: et quidquid ille mihi Hebraicis verbis expressit, hoc ego, accito notario, sermonibus Latinis exposui. Orationibus vestris mercedem hujus operis compensabo, quum gratum vobis didicero me, quod jubere estis dignati, complesse.'

Since his time nothing had been heard of a Chaldee text of Tobit; no critic, however, doubted the veracity of the

---

[1] Opera, ed. Vallarsi, Verona, 1740, t. x.

father's statement. The text which we now publish agrees
in one important point with the version of the Vulgate,
in representing Tobit in the first chapters in the third
person, whilst in all other old versions he speaks in the
first person. It is true, however, that our Chaldee text 'is
less in accordance with the Vulgate than with the other
texts, as we shall point out later on, and in many places
it differs in order and words from Jerome's translation. This, however, can be accounted for. On the
one hand, there are many omissions in our MS. of the
Chaldee text[1], and it has most likely been abridged for
adaptation to the Midrash. On the other hand, Jerome,
who translated his text in one day with the help of a
Jewish interpreter, dictating it at the same time in Latin to
his secretary, could hardly have made an accurate translation. Moreover, he made use, as is evident, of the old
Latin version, called the *Itala;* and it cannot be doubted
that he revised his translation before giving it to the public.
His method in translating Tobit, although he does not
mention it, was probably the same as that which he employed
in the translation of Judith from a Chaldee text. We quote
a part of his preface to that book[2]: 'Apud Hebraeos Liber
Judith inter Apocrypha legitur: cujus auctoritas ad robo-
randa illa quae in contentionem veniunt, minus idonea
judicatur. Chaldeo tamen sermone conscriptus, inter histo-
rias computatur. Sed quia hunc librum Synodus Nicaena
in numero sanctarum Scripturarum legitur computasse,

---

[1] See pp. 6, 7, 8, 9, and 15. On p. 8, lines 3–5, the text is even out of
order.

[2] Opera, t. x. Vallarsi already says, 'Eo fortasse, quo Tobiae versio-
nem modo adornaverat, ut quae Chaldaice scripta erant, alio in Hebraicum
reddente, ipse in Latinum refunderet, historiae magis veritatem quam
sententiarum et verborum seriem sedulo persequutus.' See also Bickell in
the Zeitschrift für Katholische Theologie, 1878, ii, p. 221.

acquievi postulationi vestrae, immo exactioni: et sepositis
occupationibus, quibus vehementer arctabar, huic unam
lucubratiunculam dedi, magis sensum e sensu quam ex
verbo verbum transferens. Multorum codicum varietatem
vitiosissimam amputavi: sola ea, quae intelligentia integra
in verbis Chaldaeis invenire potui, Latinis expressi [1].'

Accordingly, if we take into consideration the somewhat
arbitrary proceedings of the Rabbi who adapted his text
to the Midrash, and of Jerome who paid more attention to
the sense than to the words, and who evidently made
many additions (e. g. ii. 12–19, iii. 16–23, vi. 17 to end), we
may venture to say that our Chaldee text in a more complete form was the original from which the translation of
the Vulgate was made.

Before entering into details on the old versions of Tobit
and their relations to the Chaldee text, we must give
some account of our MS. It was bought at Constantinople by Herr Fischel Hirsch, bookseller at Halberstadt,
and purchased from him for the Bodleian Library. It
contains a collection of smaller and larger Midrashim [2],
copied in the fifteenth century in Greek-rabbinical characters. The book of Tobit is the fifth piece of this collection,
and is stated to be an extract from the Midrash Rabbah de
Rabbah. We know the Midrash Rabbah or Rabboth on the
Pentateuch and the five Scrolls, of which that on Genesis is

---

[1] We take the opportunity of correcting Dr. Jellinek's statement (Beth
ham-Midrash, i, p. xxiii), that the first Hebrew translation of the book of
Judith was made by R. 'Aqiba Levi in 1679. There are two earlier
translations of this book: 1. A literal one of the text of the Vulgate, made
before 1547 A.D., to be found in the MS. Opp. 712 in the Bodleian
Library (see our Catalogue, No. 2240). 2. A less literal one, printed at
Venice, about 1650 (see Steinschneider's Catal. Bodl., No. 1340, and
[Zedner's] Catalogue of the British Museum, p. 149).

[2] See our Catalogue of the Bodleian Hebrew MSS., No. 2339.

attributed to R. Osh'aya[1], but no mention whatever is
made of a Midrash Rabbah de Rabbah, either in old or
in modern works on Jewish literature.   Raymund Martini,
however, gives in his Pugio Fidei[2] a large number of
extracts from a Midrash B'reshith (i. e. on Genesis) major,
and amongst them a part of the history of Bel and the
Dragon, agreeing *verbatim* with the text here published from
our MS.[3]   In our MS. it is said to be extracted from the
Midrash Rabbah de Rabbah.   It is certain therefore that
the Midrash major on Genesis of Martini and our Midrash
Rabbah de Rabbah are identical.   Don Isaac Abarbanel[4],
who seems to have possessed a copy of this Midrash major,
quotes it under the name of B'reshith Rabba Rabbathâ or
the great B'reshith Rabbah[5].   According to our MS., however, we must call it the Midrash Rabbah of Rabbah,
i. e. attributed to Rabbah[6].   Martini gives also many
extracts from a B'reshith major on Genesis, attributed to
R. Moses had-Darshan, which Zunz[7] thinks identical with
the already-mentioned B'reshith major.   They are, however, in our opinion, two different books, for the following
reasons: I. We give on p. 36 of the text an additional
passage to the Midrash Thanhumâ, which is attributed to
R. Moses had-Darshan, referring to the history of Tobit,
though no names are given.   Now this piece has little in

---

[1] See Zunz, Die Gottesdienstlichen Vorträge der Juden, p. 174.

[2] Edition of Voisin, p. 742.   [3] See the text, p. 41.

[4] Y'shu'oth M'shiho, ed. of Carlsruhe, p. 28ᵃ and elsewhere.

[5] Our printed Midrash is called by Martini *minor* and by Abarbanel
זוטא.   Alfonso de Zamora quotes the two under the name of B'reshith
Rabbah' u-K'tanah (see Archives des Missions Scientifiques, 2nd series, t. v
(Paris, 1858), p. 428).

[6] We do not think רבה דרבה can be taken in the sense of the
Thalmudical expression רובא דרובא.   R. Jehudah Gedalyah (see Jellinek
in קונטרס תרי"ג, p. 47) quotes a Midrash רבי רבתי רבה.

[7] See below, p. xix.

common with our text of Tobit extracted from the anonymous Midrash major. 2. Don Isaac Abarbanel, as we have
stated, possessed a copy of the Midrash major, but when
he quotes the extracts from the B'reshith Rabbah of
R. Moses had-Darshan, he adds that he cannot verify
the quotation. Martini had therefore, no doubt, two
Midrashim furnished him by the Jews, either in two
distinct MSS. or in one, where the text was the Midrash
major and the marginal notes or addition by R. Moses
had-Darshan. This last was the case with the MS. of
the Midrash Rabbathi, formerly in possession of the celebrated Rapoport[1], and now in the library of the Jewish
congregation at Prague, and which Dr. Jellinek describes
as the work of R. Moses had-Darshan[2].

Our Chaldee text quoted from the Midrash Rabbah of
Rabbah, which we have identified with the B'reshith Rabbah major of Martini, would, even if we were to accept
Zunz's identification of it with the B'reshith Rabbah of
R. Moses had-Darshan, be known at all events at the
beginning of the eleventh century amongst the Jews[3].
It must, however, be much older (as might have been
argued from our distinction between the two Midrashim,
viz. the anonymous major and that of R. Moses had-
Darshan), since it is anterior to the Hebrew text published
by us, which is believed to be from the fifth to the seventh
century[4]. For the Hebrew cannot be a translation from

---

[1] See below, p. xix.

[2] Beth ham-Midrash, vi, p. xiv sqq., and קונטרס תרי"ג, p. 47. We may
add that the Agadic §§ on pp. 15 to 18 and on p. xvi of Beth ham-Midrash
are also to be found in our MS. ff. 44 and 49[b] with better readings (e. g.
on p. 18, וחצי שבט מנשה שם נגב). The Agadic § in Hebrew of i, p. 84
of the same work, is to be found in our MS. in Chaldee on p. 41.

[3] See the extract from Zunz below, p. xix.

[4] See Fritsche's Exegetisches Handbuch zu den Apocryphen, 2nd fasc.,

the Itala, as has been hitherto believed[1], but must be from
a Chaldee text similar to ours, in which, however, Tobit
speaks throughout in the first person[2]. We conclude,
therefore, that Jerome had our present Chaldee text in a
fuller form before him when he made his translation of
the book.

We have now to make brief mention of the various old
texts of the book of Tobit and their relations to one another.
We shall follow entirely Prof. Bickell's excellent article on
the subject[3]. *a.* There are three Greek versions: 1. The one
usually found in all MSS., which we shall call A; 2. The
Sinaitic text[4], called B; 3. A later text, of which only
large fragments exist[5], which we call C. *β.* Of Latin
translations, the earlier is the Itala, of which three[6] versions exist, varying considerably one from the other: *a.* The
complete text published by Pierre Sabatier[7], which we
reproduce in full, this book not being accessible to every
biblical scholar; *b.* That edited by Giuseppe Bianchini[8];

Leipz. 1853, p. 14. The Hebrew translation published by Fagius from
the edition of Constantinople, 1519, is certainly much more recent than
the Münster text. Not only from the artificial style ought Prof. Fritsche
to have known that, but also from passages like עד שהלכתי באלמנייא
(ii. 11) and the play upon the words אחי אחרון for Ἀχιάχαρος.

[1] Fritsche, loc. cit.

[2] Bickell in the *Katholische Zeitschrift*, ii, p. 219.

[3] Op. cit., pp. 217, 218.

[4] Published by Prof. Reusch in 1870.

[5] Published by Prof. Fritsche, op. cit., pp. 89–110.

[6] The library of Munich possesses an unedited version, which Dr. Ziegler
intends to publish shortly.

[7] *Bibliorum sacrorum Latinae versiones antiquae seu vetus Italica* etc.,
Paris, 1751, t. i, fol. 709 sqq. The figures agree with the Vulgate. We
have corrected a few evident clerical mistakes, and have made a few alterations in the punctuation.

[8] *Vindiciae canonicarum Scripturarum Vulgatae Latinae editionibus* etc.,
Rome, 1740, fol. 350 sqq.

c. The fragments published by Cardinal Mai[1]. γ. The Vulgate is the later translation by Jerome, which was made from a Chaldee text, the translator making large use of the Itala[2]. δ. Our Chaldee text, which agrees for the greater part with the Sinaitic text, and consequently with the Itala. However, the Chaldee text has sentences which are to be found sometimes in one, sometimes in another of the above-mentioned texts[3]; others are peculiar to the Chaldee text or the Hebrew translation. This fact alone would be sufficient to shew that the Chaldee is not a translation from one of the Greek or the Latin texts[4]; and moreover the pure Semitic idiom of the Chaldee text does not admit for a moment the possibility of its being a translation from a non-Semitic text[5]. ε. The Hebrew text which we publish is a translation from an earlier recension of our Chaldee text, which preserved the more original form, viz. Tobit speaking in the first person. In fact, many omissions

---

[1] Ex antiqua versione seu Italica vetera divinorum Librorum fragmenta (t. ix of Spicilegium Romanum), p. 21 sqq.

[2] Fr. H. Reusch, Das Buch Tobias, Freiburg, 1857, p. xxxiv.

[3] We cannot undertake to point out minutely all the differences of the various Greek and Latin texts from the Chaldee and Hebrew texts, our edition being intended to give the newly-discovered text with a faithful translation, and not an exegetical commentary on Tobit. We shall therefore quote only a few of those differences. Chap. I. אחוהי דקברי קריביה (text, p. 4, l. 5), 'the brother of Kabri his kinsman' (transl. p. xxviii), is neither in the Hebrew nor in the Vulgate. In the Itala (i. 16), 'fratri meo filio Gabahel (in *b.* et Gabin).' Greek, A. τῷ ἀδελφῷ Γαβρία, B. τοῦ Γαβρὶ τῷ ἀδελφῷ μου, C. τῷ ἀδελφῷ τῷ Γαβρεί. P. 3, l. 16, ורבת to קשישא only in the Chaldee. P. 5, l. 12, וכל צפר וצפר with Itala *b.* cotidie. See also Dr. Bickell's above-mentioned article, p. 218.

[4] The forms of Ragais or Ragas, Egbatanes or Egbatanas, and Tigrin would scarcely occur in the text if translated from the Greek or the Latin. The same may be said of the form אקיקר for Ἀχίχαρος, Ἀχειάχαρος, Ἀχίκαρος, and Achicarus.

[5] The biblical verses agree mostly with the translation of Onqelos.

and not a few corruptions in our Chaldee text, which is
published from a single MS., can be supplied and amended
from the Hebrew translation, but the Hebrew translation
has additions by the copyists, such as the enlargement of
the prayers and Midrashic application of biblical verses.
Both Chaldee and Hebrew leave out the mention of the
dog; nor have they the latter part of the thirteenth or
any portion of the fourteenth chapter. The latter omissions, however, are to be also found in a Syriac text based
on a Greek version, and in a MS. of the Itala[1]. The Hebrew
text, although shorter, agrees in the last chapters partly
with the Sinaitic text.

. We publish the Hebrew text from the first edition
printed at Constantinople in 1516, which Sebastian Münster
reproduced in 1542, and which is hence usually but wrongly
called the Münster text, as if he had been the first who
published it. This text is marked in our notes with M.
The same text, with Münster's Latin version, is to be found
in Walton's Polyglot. Collation has been made with the
following MSS.: 1. By ourselves with No. 1251 of the
Hebrew MSS. in the National Library in Paris, marked in
the notes with P. This is not an accurate copy, but some
of its variations will be found useful. On the margin are
to be found some variations from the Münster text. The
few additions in this MS. not to be found in the other
copies are distinguished by [ ]. 2. With the Persian[2]
translation of the Hebrew, written in Hebrew characters,
to be found in No. 130 of the Hebrew MSS. in the National

---

[1] See Bickell, op. cit., p. 216.

[2] According to Prof. De Lagarde (Göttinger Gelehrten Anzeige, 1877,
i, p. 742 sqq.) this translation is made in the Pehlewi idiom, which the
Jews in Persia spoke, just as now in Turkey Jews still speak Spanish
after having been exiled from Spain nearly four centuries.

Library. This translation was probably made about 1400
A. D.[1], and is only a literal and ignorant translation[2]; but
it is therefore of value for the critical arrangement of the
Hebrew text. Two of the variations are rather important, as they agree with the Vulgate[3]. We have marked
this MS. in the notes with Pr. It agrees completely
with the following text. 3. By our friend the learned
Abbate Pierre Perreau, librarian of the Royal Library of
Parma, with No. 194 of De-Rossi's Catalogue. It is marked
in our notes with Π.[4] The passages to be found in M. and
Π. and not in P. are pointed out by ( ). No division into
chapters or verses exists in the MSS. of the Chaldee and
the Hebrew versions, but we have for convenience of the
reader adopted the division into chapters according to the
Itala[5]. There are, however, some blank spaces in the MS.
which we have marked either by : or a full stop.

In order to be complete as regards the history of Tobit
in the Midrashic literature, we have added in No. III. the
passage contained in the addition to the Midrash Thanḥumâ according to the edition of Mantua. There is,
however, another reason for the addition of this text, viz.
the argument it supplies for distinguishing the anonymous

---

[1] See Munk's introduction to Isaiah in Cahen's Bible, Paris, 1838,
p. 134 sqq.

[2] See p. 19, note 8; p. 25, note 9. משכרון (text, p. 24, l. 7) 'from
drunkenness' (Itala iv. 16) is translated by از مزدوری 'from a hired la-
bourer.' בבית אל, p. 20, l. 18, بخانه خودای . He translates the following
proper names: קוסמנטנייה with ארדט ארם, בגדאד with בבל, ירואק with מדי
אשור with מוצל.

[3] P. 20, note 6; Vulg. ii. 3, de accubitu suo. P. 21, note 3; Vulg. ii.
11, ex nido.

[4] Huet (Demonstratio Evangelica, Prop. IV, de libro Tobiae) knew
either the MS. P. or Π. See also Bochart's Hierozoicon, II. v. 14, de
pisce Tobiae.

[5] The division in the Hebrew text is left according to Münster.

B'reshith Rabbah major from that of R. Moses had-Darshan.
For this reason we have also thought it necessary to add in
an appendix the history of Bel and the Dragon in the Syriac
version [1], which is given in the MS. as extracted from the
Midrash Rabbah of Rabbah, and part of which, as we have
already stated, is quoted in the Pugio Fidei as taken from
the Midrash major. The Syriac version of the Apocrypha,
transcribed in Hebrew characters, was known amongst the
Jews in Spain. Moses ben Nahman of Gerona, usually
known as Nahmanides, quotes in his commentary on the
Pentateuch passages of the Syriac version of the Wisdom
of Solomon, and the M'gillath Shushan, or the book of
Judith [2]. To this we have annexed a small passage of the
B'reshith Rabbah, or the Midrash Rabbah on Genesis, which
alludes to the history of Bel and the Dragon. We may
mention, however, that this passage is not to be found in
some MSS. of this Midrash, a statement which will be
useful for the vindication of Raymund Martini against
recent attacks upon him, which follows as a note to this
preface.

We have now to say a word about the language in
which the original book of Tobit was composed. That the
author wrote in a Semitic dialect cannot be doubted; the
earliest translations sufficiently prove this [3]. Written by
a Jew, we have only to choose between the Hebrew of
the later idiom and the Chaldee, from which last our text
would be abridged and adapted to the Midrash. We agree
here again with Dr. Bickell [4], that the original composition

---

[1] We have thought it superfluous to give a translation of it, since a Latin
translation of it is given in the Polyglot.

[2] See Zunz, op. cit., p. 123.

[3] See Reusch, Das Buch Tobias, p. xvi sqq.

[4] Op. cit., p. 219. We cannot, however, admit his conjecture (ibid.
p. 220), that the original text in vi. 16 (Vulgate 19) had תחת לבונה,

of the book was in Hebrew, although no such text is
mentioned by Origen and his contemporaries. Indeed,
proper names like Rafael, i. e. 'may God heal[1]' (with
allusion to the double healing of Tobi and Sarah), Tobi and

---

and that the Chaldee read for it לבושה and translated accordingly (p. 11,
l. 4) תחות לבישה, since this error would be impossible in the corres-
ponding passage on p. 12, l. 12. Τῇ Βάαλ in i. 5 of the Greek A is a
corruption for Beth El (text, p. 3, l. 12). Another argument for a
Hebrew original of Tobit is adduced by Prof. Graetz (Geschichte der
Juden, 2nd edition, vol. iv, p. 466), and literally translated by Dr. Ginsburg (in Kitto's Cyclopedia, art. Tobit), from the passage iv. 17, Ἔκχεον
τοὺς ἄρτους σου ἐπὶ τὸν τάφον τῶν δικαίων (Chaldee, p. 8, l. 10; Hebrew,
p. 24, l. 9), which, they say, could only be explained if we suppose the
original had שלח לחמך בקרב הצדיקים 'send forth thy bread amongst
the just;' 'the translator (Dr. Ginsburg says) by a transposition of the
last two letters having read בקבר instead of בקרב, and שפך instead of
שלח, as is evident from the antithetical clause, "and give it not to the
wicked."' The two authors might have mentioned the text of Itala b:
'Panem tuum et vinum distribue cum justis.' The emendation is, according
to our opinion, not necessary at all. In old times it was already customary
for the friends of mourners to bring them food and drink; compare 2 Sam.
iii. 35 (Ewald, Die Alterthümer des Volkes Israel, 3rd ed., p. 204). Sirach
(30. 18) and Josephus (B. J., II. i. 1) allude to the same custom (Fritsche,
op. cit., p. 46, and Perles, in Frankel's Monatsschrift, t. x, p. 394). The
Thalmud also mentions similar usages (S'mahoth, chap. 14, and Jer. Th.
B'rakhoth iii. 5). The meal of the mourners (סעורת הבראה) after
the burial, which is still in use among the Jews, is no doubt a remnant
of the ancient rite (private communication of Dr. Perles); for שפך as
well as ἐκχέειν in the sense of 'giving freely,' see Fritsche, op. cit., p. 45,
and Bab. Thalm., 'Erubin, fol. 65ª. Jerome's translation, 'constitue
panem' etc., would imply the reading אשוי instead of אשור of our
text. The emendation of מצנדרן, proposed by Dr. Kohut (Geiger's
Jüdische Zeitschrift, 1872, p. 55) for מצרים (p. 12, l. 13, and p. 29, l. 16),
cannot be admitted; see p. xvii. The problem could perhaps be solved if
we could guess what word the original might have had for χειρόγραφον,
chirographum (chaps. v. and ix), where the Chaldee and the Hebrew texts
have 'bag.' Dr. Perles proposes either חרט, which means 'writing' (Isaiah
viii. 1) as well as 'bag' (2 Kings v. 23), or the Thalmudical דיסקא (see
Levy's Neuhebräisches und Chaldäisches Lexicon, i. 400 and ii. 169, 170).

[1] See Fagius' preface to his edition of Tobit (p. x, note 1).

Tobiyyah (the former only used in later Hebrew), Gabaiel, 'treasurer of God,' Reuel, and Ednah in connection with Sarah, could only be employed by a writer in Hebrew. Most of the Apocryphal books of the Old Testament, it has now been proved by critics, were composed in Hebrew[1]. No books are more subject to additions, alterations, and various adaptations than popular histories; the text is in the hands of a few, and the contents are related orally to the people; hence the great variety in the texts, even of the early translations.

As to the object of the beautiful story of Tobit, it is in our opinion neither an admonition to observe the payment of the tithes and to give alms, according to the view of the Midrash (which Ewald has adopted without knowing the Midrash), nor an exhortation to observe the sacrifices and other laws mentioned in Leviticus. Such admonitions would be nothing new, and there would be no occasion to compose a popular history to enforce them. We believe with Prof. Graetz and Dr. Kohut, that the frequent and strange allusion to a secret burial of dead men, the special demand of Tobi to bury him and his wife in honour, the lamentation of Sarah that she had no one to bury her parents, must refer to a time when this action was prohibited to the Jews. Of this we know two periods in Jewish history: 1. In the time of the domination of the Guebres in Persia, on which ground Dr. Kohut[2] thinks that the book was composed in Persia about the time of Ardeshir I. This hypothesis has in its favour that the author places° the

---

[1] See for Judith, F. C. Movers in the Zeitschrift für Philosophie und Katholische Theologie, Köln, 1835, p. 8 sqq.; for Susanna, N. Brüll, Jahrbücher für Jüdische Geschichte, vol. iii, p. 68; for Baruch and minor treatises, Plessner, Die Apokryphischen Bücher ins Hebräische übersetzt, Berlin, 1833.

[2] Geiger's Jüdische Zeitschrift, 1872, p. 70 sqq.

scene of the history in Persian towns, and that Asmodeus
and the demons are of Persian origin. But inasmuch as
the book of Tobit is mentioned by Clemens of Alexandria
and by Polycarp, the time of Ardeshir (about 250 A.D.)
would be too late. 2. Prof. Graetz[1] puts its composition
in the time of Hadrian, after the fall of the famous fortress
of Bether, so valiantly defended by Bar-Kokhba. The Thalmud[2] mentions in fact that the benediction after meals,
'Blessed be he who is good and doeth good,' was insti-
tuted after the dead bodies round Bether were allowed
to be buried[3]. Nineveh and Babel in the later Jewish
as also the Christian literature allude always to Rome.
To this opinion we adhere; at all events the book can
scarcely have been composed earlier, since it was not
known to Josephus.

We express our best thanks to our friend Mr. H. J.
Mathews, M.A., for the revision of the proofs, and especially
for the trouble he has taken to adapt our translation to the
English of the authorised version[4]. We have also to
thank M. Delisle, Member of the French Institute and
Director of the National Library in Paris, for the loan of
the MS. containing the Persian translation.

A. N.

Oxford,
April, 1878.

---

[1] Geschichte der Juden (2nd edition), vol. iv, p. 466.

[2] Babyl. Th., Tha'anith, fol. 31ᵃ and elsewhere, mentioned in the name
of a late authority (Graetz, l. c.)

[3] משנתנו הרוגי בתר לקבורה נקבעה הטוב והמטיב. It is possible
that הטוב והמטיב has some connection with the names טוביה בן טובי.

[4] The emendation on p. 15, note 3, is due to Dr. W. Wright of Cambridge,
and that on p. 16, note 1, to Dr. Perles of Munich.

NOTE ON

RAYMUND MARTINI'S PUGIO FIDEI.

WE have had to quote the Pugio Fidei in connection with the Midrash out of which the Chaldee text of Tobit and the Syriac text of Bel and the Dragon are taken. In relying upon Martini's authority we are bound, contrary to our will, to defend him against the attack made lately upon him in calling him a forger and an impostor[1]. At the time when Dr. Pusey wrote his preface to the English translation of the texts of the Fifty-third Chapter of Isaiah according to the Jewish Interpreters, in which he breaks a lance on behalf of the author of the Pugio Fidei, we had not examined the manuscript out of which we publish Tobit, and therefore could not provide him with the materials which we have now at our disposal. Dr. Pusey's defence of Martini is therefore based only on internal grounds. His conclusion is the following[2]: 'Amid the various sources of human mistake, we are bound by the duties of our common humanity not to assume the very worst, dishonesty; but to believe what a person says that he saw with his own eyes. Enough has been said, perhaps, where demonstration on either side is impossible, since the extracts were made nearly six centuries ago, and the MSS. which Martini had before him have long since perished.'

Dr. Zunz, whom Dr. Pusey overlooked, wrote in the same strain some forty years ago. In his unsurpassed book on the Agadah he speaks of R. Moses had-Darshan's Midrash and the Pugio Fidei in the following terms[3]: 'R. Moses had-Darshan of Narbonne, the teacher of R. Nathan[4], and so belonging to

---

[1] See below, p. xx.
[2] The Fifty-third Chapter of Isaiah according to the Jewish Interpreters, Oxford, 1877, vol. ii, p. xxxv.
[3] Die Gottesdienstlichen Vorträge der Juden, Berlin, 1832, p. 287 sqq.
[4] Of Rome, the celebrated author of the Thalmudical Dictionary, called 'Arukh.

the third quarter of the eleventh century, is known from quotations in the Arukh, Rashi, Thosafoth, Mord'khai, and the additions
to the Thanḥumâ, as the author of elucidations of Thalmudic
passages and different books of the Bible. His commentary on
the Scriptures gives partly explanations of the language and
matter, and partly older Agadahs and original expositions in
the Agadic style. The investigation of the works of R. Moses
is peculiarly intricate, owing to the following circumstance. The
monk Raymund Martini quotes in his Pugio Fidei a considerable
number of passages out of "the great B'reshith Rabbah of
R. Moses had-Darshan," which for the most part, sometimes in
the original and sometimes in the Latin translation, have been
again copied from Martini by Porchet, Joshua of Lorca, and
Peter Galatin in their works. No such work, however, is any-
where named in Jewish authors; since Abarbanel, who gives
extracts from it, simply refutes the objections of Joshua of
Lorca, and himself acknowledges that he did not possess the
great B'reshith Rabbah[1]. This circumstance might make the
existence of such a Midrash altogether suspicious, if there were
not strong reasons in favour of it. It is by no means extra-
ordinary that the mention of a whole work has been preserved
in one single author alone; besides, the harmonious character
of the fragments, and also the positive marks of their origin—
of which neither Martini nor anybody else could have had a
misgiving—speak in favour of the existence of that Midrash.
Many of the extracts adduced are also to be found in Agadahs
of a different kind, and thus it would have been as unnecessary
as impossible to expressly forge a work of this kind. Finally,
Martini was neither an apostate, like Joshua, nor a liar, like
Galatin, but a deeply-learned man, who did not require to
strengthen his numerous extracts from well-known Halakhic
and Agadic writings with the addition of fraud. We are therefore obliged to acknowledge the genuineness of that great B'reshith Rabbah, and it only remains for criticism to decide whether
R. Moses is the author, or whether any particular part has been
interpolated. The whole of this investigation has taken a completely new direction, since the actual discovery of a *B'reshith
Rabbathi* in the original[2]. From the communications made to
me on this subject, it follows that much therein agrees with
the fragments in Martini, other parts with the character of the

---

[1] See, however, above, p. viii.   [2] See above, p. ix.

explanations preserved by Rashi; much, however, especially
the passages controverted by Abarbanel, is missing. I am of
opinion that the work of R. Moses was put forth after his time
with additions under the name B'reshith Rabbathi, and that the
same was in the hands of the interpolator of the Thanhumâ and
perhaps R. Isaac Nathan[1]. To the author of the Yalqut it was
probably only imperfectly known. In relation to this greater collection Martini calls *our* B'reshith Rabbah the little or short.'

The Revs. A. C. Jennings and W. H. Lowe (for they claim
a joint production[2] in the appendix which is intended to 'triumph
over a dead lion,' as Dr. Pusey says of Martini in a private
communication) are of another opinion concerning Martini. We
shall quote their own words[3]: 'The reader is warned against
accepting as genuine the citations from Jewish works in Schoettgen's Horae Hebraicae and Raymund Martini's Pugio Fidei.
Both works are utterly untrustworthy. Raymund Martini
(Ordinis Praedicatorum adversus Mauros et Judaeos, fl. cir.
1250) is notorious for the questionable expedients which he
adopted in endeavouring to refute the Jews from their own
books. With that well-meaning dishonesty which too fre-
quently marked the controversialists of his age, he alters the
text of the Talmud, Midrashim, etc., to meet his occasion, and
even devises whole passages where convenient. Martini was a
sound Hebrew scholar, and as his forgeries are generally clever
adaptations and combinations from other parts of Hebrew literature, it is only by reference to the actual texts of these Jewish works
that his impostures are betrayed.' We do not think that any
accusation of literary fraud could be expressed in stronger terms
than those which the two commentators on the Psalms have
chosen. Had they known Zunz's excellent book, they would
have perhaps modified their language, and at all events not
have said that Martini (we leave Schoettgen to his fate) ' is
notorious for his questionable expedients.' Moreover, they
would have learned from Zunz that the result of their 'joint
production' is nothing new, since Don Isaac Abarbanel[4], in

---

[1] He seems to have written about 1450 an apologetical work against
Yoshu'a of Lorca or Hieronymus de Sancta Fide.

[2] The Psalms with Introduction and Critical Notes, London, 1877, at
the beginning.

[3] Appendix to Psalm CX.

[4] Y'shuoth M'shiḥo, ed. Carlsruhe.

calling Hieronymus de Sancta Fide an impostor and forger,
strikes with the same blow Martini, for both quote the same
passages[1]. From Abarbanel's book also they could have quoted,
without needing much research, many instances which would have
supported their case better. On the other hand, they would have
seen from Zunz that the B'reshith Rabbah quoted by Martini is
not the printed book we have, but quite a distinct work. And
so they would have had no occasion to say, 'We cannot find
that the comments on vv. 3, 4, quoted in the P. F. as from the
Bereshith Rabba, have any existence in that work, nor do we
believe that they were in former times discoverable there.'

But let us now take up the other passages, besides those of
the B'reshith Rabbah, given jointly by the two learned clergymen. 'His note,' they say, 'on the first verse of the Targum
of Psalm cx is a fair sample of Martini's comments, "Targum
[pro במימריה !] למימריה 'יי אמר *Dixit Dominus Verbo suo.* . . .
Notandum valde est quod Targum dicit, *Dixit Dominus Verbo
suo* ubi David dixit, *Dixit Dominus Domino meo.*" [Pugio
Fidei, 554. Let the student compare both Targums.]' We,
confess that it is a bad case for Martini, for למימריה is without
example in the Thargums, where we always find במימריה[2], although
it is not impossible that some ignorant copyist may have written
למימריה to accord with the ל of לאדני. But we are sorry to say
that it is an equally bad case for the two learned authors, that
they should not have seen on the margin of the Pugio Fidei
a note by Voisin[3], that the Barcelona and Majorca MSS. of this
work (those are the oldest and the best) have not the passage at
all, and it is therefore a later addition. How this oversight has
happened to authors who state, 'It is most unfortunate that
modern commentators have so readily relied on these two autho-
rities. In our Introduction we depend upon no passages but
such as we have ourselves verified,' we are not bound to
explain.

They say further on, 'We may instance also Martini's auda-
cious alteration of the text of Siphra d'Rab, D'boore Y'hovah,

---

[1] To judge from the Latin text of S. Fide's Hebraeomastix there are
some variations between the two texts. The quotations in Abarbanel,
however, agree with those of Martini.

[2] See Maybaum, Die Anthropomorphismen und Anthropopathien bei
Onkelos, etc., Breslau, 1870, p. 47.

[3] Pugio Fidei, p. 554.

xii. 20.' We have said elsewhere[1] that the Messianic words
read by Martini in the Siphrâ are not to be found either in the
editions or in the Bodleian MS. But it is possible and probable
that in Martini's and S. Fide's MSS. of the book there was a
later addition, a gloss, for instance, which passed into the text.
We really do not see Martini's necessity for forging a Messianic
passage, the substance of which he could have found elsewhere.
If, however, he did quote from works which did not exist, he
did it in the best of company, that of our two learned authors.
They quote from a דבורא יהוה, which exists neither in print nor
in MS. Can they mean the דבורא דחובא ?

Do Messrs. Jennings and Lowe believe that the Jews who had
to furnish Martini with MSS. would not in their controversy
have told him that he falsified passages, as Moses ben Naḥman
of Gerona intended to do with Paulus Christianus[2], when he
asked him to shew him the books out of which he quoted[3]?
The books were handed over to him, but the quotations were
right. Abarbanel[4] cries out against the Rabbis contemporary
with Hieronymus de Sancta Fide, asking them why they did
not, instead of arguing with him, produce their books and shew
him that he was an impostor. They did so in one instance
only, and they did it not in other instances for the simple
reason that Hieronymus quoted rightly. That one instance is
the following passage quoted from the B'reshith Rabbah[5]: 'Et
Melchizedek rex Salem (Gen. xiv. 18). Iste erat Sem filius
Noae. Et quid docet dicendum, produxit panem et vinum ?
R. Samuel bar Nahman dixit, Sentencias sacerdotii tradidit ei,
et ipse erat sacrificans panem, et vinum Deo, sicut dictum est
Gen. xiv. 18. Et ipse erat Sacerdos Dei altissimi, etc. Rex.

---

[1] The Fifty-third Chapter of Isaiah, etc., vol. ii, p. 5. S. Fide (i. 11)
quotes rightly the Siphrâ (Zifrat), apparently from another MS. Dr.
Wünsche in his book, Die Leiden des Messias, Leipzig, 1870, p. 65, gives
a reference to the Siphré, p. 121. Which edition? It is astonishing that
Abarbanel did not cry out against this passage; he surely possessed the
Siphrâ.

[2] See Histoire Littéraire de la France, t. xxvii, p. 563 sqq.

[3] Vikkuaḥ (Disputatio), ed. Steinschneider, Berlin, 1860, p. 19.

[4] Op. cit., p. 36ᵃ.

[5] We quote according to Martini, Pugio Fidei, p. 654 (chap. de Sacra-
mento Eucharistiae). In Hieronymus (Hebraeomastix. i. 9) the passage is
not complete. Abarbanel's quotation (fol. 47) agrees with Martini. Dr.
Perowne's quotations agree neither with Martini nor with Hieronymus.
What is his authority?

Salem. Locus quandoque justificat habitatores suos. Aliter.
Producit panem : hic est panis propositionis, *et vinum* i. e. liba-
mina. Magistri dixerunt quod revelavit ei legem, sicut dictum
est Prov. ix. 5. *Venite, comedite panem meum, et bibite vinum
quod miscui.* Aliter. *Melchizedek,* hoc est ac si dixerit scrip-
tura quod dictum est Ps. cx. 4: *Juravit Dominus, et non
poenitebit eum; Sacerdos tu ad saeculum secundum ordinem
Melchizedek.* Et quis est iste ? Iste est rex justus, et salvator
Rex Messias, de quo dictum est Zach. ix. 9: *Ecce rex tuus venit
tibi justus, et Salvator.* Et quid docet dicendum, *Protulit panem
et vinum?* quasi dicat, *Placenta tritici in terra,* Ps. lxxii. 16.
Et hoc est quod dictum Gen. xiv. 18: Et ipse erat Sacerdos
altissimi.' Hieronymus has instead of 'Et ipse erat sacrificans
panem et vinum Dei' (p. xxii, l. 28), the following words : 'Qui
erat panem et vinum sacrificare.' The Rabbis contemporary with
Hieronymus said, according to Abarbanel[1], that those words are
not to be found in the passage quoted from the B'reshith Rabbah,
but they did not deny the existence of the passage entirely.
Now the two learned clergymen say with reference to the same
passage : ' That the Bereshith Rabba would unconsciously furnish
arguments for the doctrines of the Immaculate Incarnation and
the Eucharist is hardly probable ; that Martini would be ready
to father passages on Bereshith Rabba appears likely from his
procedure elsewhere.'

We have no complete copy of the B'reshith Rabbah major, but
in the collection contained in our MS. (ff. 40^b and 47^b) we find
verbatim the passages of the Pugio Fidei beginning ויצא יעקב
(fol. 601), with the marginal readings, and that beginning והיה
בכל (fol. 280)[2]. We have seen also[3] that the history of Bel and
the Dragon, quoted partly by Martini from the B'reshith Rabbah,
is to be found verbatim in our MS. as a quotation from the
Midrash Rabbah of Rabbah.

We have no means of contradicting all the charges of forgery
which Abarbanel makes against Hieronymus de Sancta Fide,
and implicitly against Martini. Their MSS., as we have already
stated, are not at our command, and probably never will be.
The destruction of Hebrew and Arabic MSS. has been made in
Spain wholesale. But *crimine ab uno disce omnes.* The words
נאם ה׳ לאדוני שב לימיני, which Abarbanel says[4] he did not find

---

[1] Op. cit., p. 47°.　　　[2] See Abarbanel, op. cit., p. 28ᵃ.
[3] See above, p. viii.　　　[4] Op. cit., p. 40ᵃ.

in his copies, we read in the MS. Opp. 22, fol. 66, which is a
collection of Midrashim on the Psalms by Makhir ben Abba-
Mari[1], as a quotation from the Midrash Thillim, where the
passage runs verbatim as quoted by Martini[2]. The passage
quoted by S. Fide[3] from the M'khilthâ, with reference to which
Abarbanel[4] accuses him of having mixed up two Agadic passages
from two different Midrashim, is to be found *verbatim* in the
Midrash Sh'moth Rabbah[5]. Martini[6] quotes distinctly from the
two Midrashim. The confusion between M'khilthâ and Midrash
Sh'moth Rabbah can easily be accounted for, both being Agadic
commentaries on Exodus. The other so-called forgeries may
turn out to be genuine when some other MSS. come to light
in later time, or even from some Midrashic passages scattered
through various printed books, and hitherto not sufficiently
noticed.

---

[1] Our Catalogue of the Hebrew MSS. in the Bodleian Library, No. 167.
[2] Pugio Fidei, ff. 381 and 431.
[3] Op. cit., i. 10.
[4] Op. cit., p. 47[d].
[5] Exodus xii. 43.
[6] Op. cit., pp. 366, 367.

I. TRANSLATION OF THE CHALDEE.

THE HISTORY OF TOBIYYAH.

It is written in the Midrash Rabbah of Rabbah, in the
section beginning 'And Jacob went out' (Gen. xxviii. 10), in the
seventieth section, on the passage 'And of all that thou shalt
give me I will surely give the tenth unto thee' (Gen. xxviii. 22).
'Thou shalt truly tithe' (Deut. xiv. 22). Moses said to them,
'Ye shall receive ten blessings if ye give the tenth.' And so
Jacob said, 'And of all that thou shalt give me I will surely
give the tenth unto thee.' The ten blessings which thou shalt
give me according as my father hath blessed me, on what merit
will it be? On the merit of 'I will surely give the tenth
unto thee.'

CHAPTER I.

The history is told of a pious man whose name was Tobi, the
son of Tobiel, of the tribe of Naphthali, who was led captive in
the days of Shalmaneser, king of Assyria, and dwelt at Thisbe, a
town of Naphthali, which is in Galilee. Now Tobi walked all his
days in the right way, and he did many almsdeeds to his brethren
and his nation who were with him in the captivity in Nineveh
in the land of Assyria. And when he was but young in the
land of Israel, all the tribe of Naphthali rebelled against the
kingdom of David, and refused to go to Jerusalem. And they
sacrificed to the calves which Jeroboam, king of Israel, had
made at Bethel and Dan. And he alone went to Jerusalem at
the times of the feasts, as it is written in the book of the law of
Moses. And he brought thither the firstfruits and the heave-

offering and the tithes, and gave them to the priests and Levites,
to every one as it was meet to him, and ate the second tithe and
the poor tithe, and gave according as everything is written in
the book of Moses. And this Tobi was left an orphan by his
father, and Deborah his father's mother brought him up, and
she led him in the true path. And when he became a man he
took a wife of his own kindred, whose name was Hannah, and
she bare him a son, and he called his name Tobiyyah. Now
when Tobi was carried away captive he dwelt at Nineveh the
great city. And all his brethren and kindred polluted themselves, and did eat the bread of the sons of the Gentiles. But
he ate not, because he feared God and loved him with all his
heart. And therefore God gave him grace and favour in the
eyes of Shalmaneser, king of Assyria, and he set him master over
all that he had to the day of his death. And at that time he committed to the hand of Gabael, the brother of Kabri his kinsman,
at the city Rages in the land of Media, ten talents of silver. And
in the days of Tobi, Shalmaneser, king of Assyria, died, and Sennacherib his son reigned in his stead. And in those days the
tribute became great, and Tobi could not go to the land of
Media, for the travellers ceased by reason of the trouble, and he
did not take the money from the hand of Gabael. And in the
days of Sennacherib he did many almsdeeds to the poor, and he
fed the hungry and the orphans, and clothed the naked, and
performed many acts of kindness. And when he saw one slain,
cast out in the street of the Jews, he buried him. Now when
Sennacherib returned with confusion of face from Judah, he
went to Nineveh in fierce wrath against the ten tribes which
were in the land of Assyria, and killed many of them, and their
corpses were cast out in the street, and none buried them.
When Tobi saw that, he was sore displeased therewith, and he
rose in the night, and stole their corpses, and buried them.
And thus he did many times. Once Sennacherib sought for
the bodies of the slain, but found them not. And the men
of Nineveh went and informed the king of Tobi that it was

he who had buried them. The king commanded that he should be put to death. When Tobi heard it, he arose and fled. And then the king commanded that they should spoil his house. But he hid before him five and forty days, until that Adrammelech and Sharezer his sons killed him with the sword, and they fled into the land of Kardu, and Esarhaddon his son reigned in his stead. And the king Esarhaddon appointed Akikar, the son of Hamael, his brother, over all his affairs, and he reigned over all the land of Assyria. And Akikar spake good words to the king for Tobi, and he begged of him, so that he brought him back to Nineveh, for Akikar was his friend and kinsman. And at that time they restored to him Hannah his wife and Tobiyyah his son.

CHAPTER II.

Now it came to pass that, when the feast of weeks came, there was a plentiful meal prepared, and as he sat at the table he said to his son Tobiyyah, Go and bring to me of our poor brethren, of such as fear God, to eat with us, and I tarry for thee until thou comest. Then Tobiyyah went and found a man slain, cast out in the street, and he told his father of it. When Tobi heard this, he rose from the table and did not eat, but went and lifted him up from the street of the city, and brought him into a house until the going down of the sun, that he might be able to bury him. And he returned to his house, and ate his bread with lamentation and mourning. And he said, Woe that [that prophecy of Amos] is fulfilled in us, 'And I will turn your feasts into mourning.' And he wept very sore. And when the sun went down he went and buried him. But his kinsmen mocked him, saying, This man feareth not for his soul, and he burieth the dead ! And on that night he did not wash [himself clean of pollution] from the dead, and he laid upon his bed by the side of the wall, and his face was uncovered, and he knew not that there were birds standing above him on the wall, and some of their dung fell upon his eyes, and a whiteness came in his eyes. And every morning he went to the physicians to cure his eyes, and he was not cured, but the whiteness increased in his eyes until he became blind. And he was blind four years. And all his brethren and kindred were grieved for him, and Akikar did nourish him. Many days his wife Hannah did work for other women. And they gave her a kid for her wages. And he heard the kid crying in the house, and he asked her, From whence hast thou this kid? it is perhaps stolen, render it to its owner, for it is not lawful for us to eat of anything that is stolen. She answered him, It is not a stolen thing, but for the wages of the work of mine hands I received it. But Tobi did not believe the matter, and quarrelled with her concerning the kid. Hannah his wife answered and said to him, Where are thy good deeds and thine alms? but thy reproach is manifest to all.

CHAPTER III.

When Tobi heard this he was much grieved and did weep, and began to pray in the anguish of his soul, saying thus : Thou art righteous, O great God, and all thy works are might, and all thy ways are goodness and truth, and thou art the judge of all the earth. Punish me not according to my sins and according to the sins of my fathers, for I and my fathers have sinned before thee, and we have transgressed thy commandments, and thou hast delivered us unto captivity and for a spoil and a reproach and a proverb to all the nations amongst whom thou hast exiled us. And now, O God, thy mercy is manifold and thy judgment is true, reward me not according to my sin, but deal with me according to thy great mercy, and take my soul out of mine hands, for it is better for me to die than to live in great misery and in this reproach, so shall I no more hear shame. And the same day Sarah, the daughter of Reuel, who lived at Agbatanis, a city in the land of Media, heard a great reproach, because she had been given to seven men to wife, and no man came in unto her according to the way of all the earth, for Asmodeus, king of the demons, killed them before they came in unto her according

to the way of all the earth.   A maid said to her, It is thou who
hast·killed thine husbands, for thou hast been given to seven
husbands, and not one of them came in unto thee, for thou dost
beat them.   And for the husbands thou hast killed mayest thou
die as they have died, and may we not see of thee either son
or daughter for ever.   And it came to pass, when Sarah heard
these words, that she was very sorrowful and wept.   And she
went up to her father's upper chamber, and wished to hang herself and to bring the old age of her father with sorrow unto
the grave [1].   [And she said, I am the only daughter of my
father;] it is not good therefore for me to hang myself,
but it is better for me to pray before God and I shall hear
no more reproach.   At that time she spread out her hands in
prayer before God, and said thus : Blessed art thou, O Lord
God, merciful and gracious, and blessed is thy holy name which
is wonderful in all the world.   Let all the works of thine hand
bless thee for ever and ever.   And now, O Lord, I lift before
thee my face, and mine eyes are fixed on thee.   Bid me return
to my dust, that I may hear no more my reproach.   It is manifest to thee, O Lord, that I am pure from all pollution with
man, and that I have not polluted my name nor the name of my
father in the land of my dwelling.   I am the only daughter of
my father, neither hath he son to inherit his property, nor hath
he kinsman to whom he may leave me.   And behold seven
husbands are dead for my sake, and what more is my life
to me ?   But if it please thee not to kill me, have pity on me
that I hear reproach no more.   On that day the prayer of
them both went up before the throne of glory of the great God.
And he sent the angel Raphael to heal them twain, [that is] to
take away the whiteness from Tobi's eyes, and to give Sarah, the
daughter of Reuel, for a wife to Tobiyyah, the son of Tobi, and to
take away Asmodeus, the king of the demons, from her.   And
when Tobi had finished his prayer he returned to his house, and

---

[1] Lacuna in the text.

Sarah, the daughter of Reuel, came down from her father's upper chamber when she had made an end of praying.

CHAPTER IV.

At that time Tobi remembered the money which he had committed to the hands of Gabael in the city Rages in the land of Media. And he said within himself, Behold I have asked that my soul might die. I will call my son Tobiyyah, and will signify him of the matter of the money before I die. And he called his son Tobiyyah, and said to him, My son, when I am dead, bury me with honour, and honour thy mother, and forsake her not all the days of her life, and do for her all that is right in her eyes, and oppose not the word of her mouth. Remember what pain she suffered for thee, and when she is dead, bury her by me in one grave. And fear the Lord thy God all thy days, and let not thy will be set to sin, and transgress not the commandments. Do uprightly all thy days, and walk not with a violent man. For if thou deal truly it will be well with thee in all that thou possessest, and all who do uprightly happy are they. My son, give alms of thy substance, and do not hide thee from a poor man, so God will not hide his Majesty from thee. My son, as far as it is in the power of thine hand to give alms, give, even if riches are far from thee. Give alms, and thou shalt acquire a good treasure for the day of wrath, for it doth deliver from death, and suffereth not him that giveth it to descend into darkness: [almsgiving] is good, and whoso exerciseth it shall subsist by it. Is it not that our fathers were praised only for almsgiving? Of Abraham our father scripture declares, 'For I know him that he will command his children and his household after him . . . to do justice [or to give alms] and judgment' (Gen. xviii. 19); of Isaac it is written, 'Then Isaac sowed in that land' (Gen. xxvi. 12); of Jacob it is written, 'And of all that thou shalt give me I will surely give the tenth unto thee' (Gen. xxviii. 22). My son, keep thyself from all counsel of sinners and from all whoredom, and take thee a wife of thine own kindred, and take not from the sons of the Gentiles, for we are children of the prophets, for the first prophets were Noah, Abraham, Isaac, and Jacob, our fathers from the beginning. Remember that all these took wives from the seed of their brethren, and were blessed in their children, and their seed inherited the land. Now therefore, my son, love thy brethren, and let not thy heart be lifted up against the sons and daughters [of thy people], for in pride is much trouble, and it removeth from God[1]. My son, give thy heart to all thy work, and what is hateful to thee do not thou to others. Let not the wages of him that is hired abide with thee all night, and thy labour God will repay thee. Give of thy bread to the hungry, and of thy garments give to the naked, and let it not be hard in thine eyes. My son, spend freely[2] thy bread and wine on the burial of the just, and hearken to good counsel at all times. Ask thy God, and he will direct thy paths, for there is no good counsellor to man but God, for whom he will he lifteth up, and whom he will he humbleth. My son, keep the words of my mouth and my commandments, and let them not depart from thine eyes. And now, my son, I signify to thee of the matter of my money, ten talents that I committed to the hand of Gabael at the city Rages in Media, for I know not the day of my death. Now therefore fear God, and keep thyself from all sin, and walk with him in humbleness, and he will give thee great riches.

CHAPTER V.

Tobiyyah answered his father, All that thou hast commanded me I will do; but how can I receive the money from the hand of Gabael, who knoweth me not, and I know not him? And what sign shall I give him so that he may believe me, and give me the money? And I know not the way that leadeth me to Media. Tobi answered and said to Tobiyyah, My son, here is a sign for thee. His bag he gave me, and I gave him mine when I put the money in his hand to keep. And from that day

---

[1] Transposed in the text.   [2] See p. xiv, note 4.

to this it is twenty years. And now, my son, seek thee a trusty
man who may go with thee, and I will give him his wages.
Go, my son, while I yet live, and receive the money. So
Tobiyyah went to seek a man who might go with him, and he
found the angel Raphael standing by. But he knew not that
he was an angel of the Lord. He asked him, From whence art
thou ? He answered him, From the children of Israel, one of
thy brethren. Tobiyyah said to him, Knowest thou how to go
to Media ? The angel said to him, I know the way, and in
Media I have been the guest of our brother Gabael, who dwelleth
at [Rages, a town of Media, and it is a two days' journey from][1]
Agbatanis to Rages, and it is built on the mountain, but Agbatanis in the plain. Tobiyyah said to him, Tarry for me a little,
and I will tell my father that I desire that thou shouldest go
with me, and I will give thee the wages for the journey. He said
to him, I will stay until thou comest. Tobiyyah went and told
his father, I have found a man of our brethren who will go with
me. Tobi said to him, Go, call him, that I may know of what
tribe he is, whether he be a trusty man to go with thee.
Tobiyyah went out and called him. And Raphael went to Tobi
and said to him, Peace be to thee. Tobi said, Is it peace to me ?
why hath all this befallen me ? for I see not the light of heaven,
the sound of words I hear, but the man I see not, and I lie in
darkness. Raphael said, God is able to heal thine eyes, for thou
art a pious man. Tobi said to him, My son Tobiyyah desireth
to go to Media ; canst thou go with him, and I will give thy
wages ? He said to him, I can ; I am a messenger, and I know the
ways, and the boundaries and the mountains are known to me.
Tobi said, Tell me of what tribe thou art, and the name of the
town where thou dwellest. Raphael said to him, If I am not
right in thine eyes, go and seek another man who may go with
thy son. Tobi said to him, My brother, be not provoked with
me that I wish to know of a certainty thy name and of what

---

[1] Lacuna in the text. The translation is according to the Hebrew of M.

family thou art. He said to him, I am Azaryah, the son of
Hananel, of the family of the great Salmiyyah, of thy brethren.
Then Tobi said quietly and tranquilly, Come, my brother, be not
angry with me because I have enquired to know thy family, for
behold my brother is of a good family, and I know Hananel and
Nathan, the two sons of the great Salmiyyah, as they went
with me to Jerusalem when I dwelt in the land of Israel,
and worshipped with me there, and these were not seduced at
the time when our brethren erred. Thou art of a good family,
go in peace, and I will give thee thy wages, a drachm every day,
and thy food the same as for my son, and I will add to thy
wages [if the Lord bring you back in peace]. Raphael answered,
Fear not, for I will go with thy son, and we shall return in
peace. Tobi called his son Tobiyyah, saying to him, My son,
prepare thyself, and go on the journey with thy brother; may
the God of heaven lead you there in peace, and send his angel
with you, and prosper your journey, and bring you back in
peace. Tobiyyah kissed his father and his mother, and they
said to him, Go in peace. And they went out to go away.
Then his mother wept, and said to Tobi, Wherefore is it thou
hast not feared to send away the young man, for he is our only
son, who goeth out and cometh in before us? God hath kept us
without the money. Tobi said to her, Be not afraid, he will go
in peace, and he will return in peace, and the good angel will go
with him, and his journey will be prosperous, and thine eyes
shall see him return in peace. So make an end of weeping.

CHAPTER VI.

The young man went and Raphael with him. And they
came in the evening to the river Tigris, and they passed the
night there. And Tobiyyah ran to the river to wash his feet,
and a fish came suddenly out of the river, and devoured the
young man's bread, and the young man cried out. Raphael
said to him, Take the fish, and do not let it go. And he laid
hold of the fish, and drew it to land. Raphael said to him,

Open the fish in the middle, and take out its heart, it is good to
smoke thereof before a man in whom the spirit of a demon and
an evil spirit is, and they will flee from him; also the gall, to
anoint therewith the eyes in which whiteness is, and they shall
be healed. So Tobiyyah did, and took out the heart and the
gall, and roasted the fish, and ate, and he left the remainder
on the road. And they went to Media and came to Agbatanis.
Then Raphael said to Tobiyyah, My brother, thou comest to stay
with Reuel, who is an old man, and hath a daughter who is
exceeding fair, whose name is Sarah. And I will speak to him
that he may give her to thee to wife. And she is the only
child of her father, and he loveth her much. And she is a
good woman and feareth heaven. And when we return from
Rages we will celebrate the marriage. For I know that Reuel
will not oppose thy desire, and that he will give her to thee,
and we shall bring her with us to thy father. Tobiyyah said to
Raphael, I have heard that she hath been given to seven men,
and they died before they came in unto her; and I have heard
that Asmodeus, the king of the demons, killed them. And now
I fear the demon, lest peradventure he kill me, and I shall
bring the old age of my parents with sorrow to the grave, and
they have no other son nor daughter to bury them when they
are dead. Raphael said to him, Dost thou not remember thy
father's precept which he gave thee, that thou shouldest marry
a wife of the family of thy father? Now therefore hear me, and
fear not the demon. I know that thou shalt take her to wife
this night. And when thou shalt come into the marriage-
chamber with her, take the heart of the fish, and smoke thereof
under her garment. And the demon shall smell it, and he shall
run away, and never come again. And when thou desirest to
approach her, rise up both of you from the bed, and pray and
ask for mercy from God, who hath commanded upon you his
kindness, and who will give you healing. And thus thou shalt
approach her, and beget from her children. Fear not, for she
is appointed unto thee from the beginning, and thou shalt

deliver her from the demon.. When Tobiyyah had heard these words, the love for Sarah entered his heart.

CHAPTER VII.

And they came to the house of Reuel at Agbatanis, and they found him by the door of his house, and they saluted him. He said to them, Go in peace into the house. And they went into the house. Reuel said to Ednah his wife, How like is this young man to Tobi my brother! Ednah asked them, From whence are ye? They answered her, From the captivity which is in Nineveh, of the tribe of Naphthali. She said to them, Do ye know Tobi our brother? They said to her, We know that he is in good health. Tobiyyah said, Tobi is my father. Reuel ran towards him, and embraced him, and kissed him, and they wept. Reuel said, Blessed be Tobi, thou art the son of a righteous and honest man. The hands of pious men are weakened when a righteous man who hath done almsdeeds and many commandments is stricken blind. And Reuel embraced Tobiyyah, his brother's son, and wept on his neck. And Ednah his wife and Sarah his daughter wept upon him. Reuel killed a ram, and they prepared for them a meal, and they ate and drank. Before they had finished eating, Tobiyyah said to Raphael, Speak with Reuel concerning his daughter Sarah, that he may give her to me to wife. Raphael communicated to Reuel the words of Tobiyyah. Reuel answered Tobiyyah, My son, I know that it is better that I should give her to thee than that I should give her to another man; nevertheless I will declare unto thee the truth. I have given her already to seven men, and they died all before they came in unto her. But now eat and drink. Tobiyyah said, I will not eat till thou hast given her to me. Reuel said, Then take her, for thou art her brother, and she is thy sister, and now she is given to thee to wife after the rule of the law of Moses. May the Lord God of heaven preserve you this night, and bestow upon you his goodness and his peace. Then Reuel led his daughter Sarah, and gave her to Tobiyyah

to wife, saying to him, Take her according to the rule of the
law of Moses, and lead her away to thy father. And Reuel
called Ednah his wife to bring paper to write thereon the deed
of marriage to his daughter, and she did so, and they wrote the
deed, and witnesses signed it. And they ate and drank. Reuel
said to Ednah his wife, Prepare a bed-chamber, and bring thy
daughter, and she did so. And Ednah embraced her daughter
Sarah and wept, saying, My daughter, may the God of heaven
shew kindness to thee this night, and watch over thee, and give
thee joy for the sorrow thou hast had in time past.

CHAPTER VIII.

And it came to pass, when they had finished preparing the
chamber and the bed, that Tobiyyah and Sarah his wife went in
thither. And Tobiyyah remembered the words of Raphael, and
took the heart of the fish, and put it upon a pan, and smoked
under Sarah's garment. And Asmodeus received the smell and
fled into the utmost parts of the land of Egypt, and Raphael
imprisoned and bound him there. And they went out of the
room, and shut the door behind them. Then Tobiyyah rose from
the bed and said to Sarah, My sister, arise, and let us make supplication before God, who hath commanded his mercy and goodness
upon us. And Tobiyyah prayed before God, saying, Blessed art
thou, O Lord God of Israel, and blessed is thy name for ever;
let the heavens and all thy creatures bless thee. Thou didst
create Adam, and gavest him Eve his wife for a helper, and of them
are all the sons of men. And thou hast said, It is not good that
man should be alone, I will make him an aid like unto himself.
And now, O God, thou knowest I take not this my sister for
lust, but according to the rule of the law. Be merciful unto us,
and give us thy goodness, that we may be united in peace, and
give us good children. And Sarah answered and said, Amen. And
he went in unto her that night. Now it came to pass in the middle
of the night that Reuel arose, and bade his servants dig a grave in
the night, saying to them, If the young man die we will bury

him in the night, so that no man know it, and there will be no
reproach to us. And he called his wife Ednah, and said to her,
Send one of the maids to the chamber with a light in her hand, and
let her see whether he be alive ; if he be not, then we will bury
him, and no man shall perceive it. And Ednah sent her maid
to the chamber, and she looked, and behold they were both of them
asleep, and she came forth and told them, Bless ye the master of
the world, for he is alive. Then Reuel said, Blessed art thou, O
Lord God of heaven and earth, thou dost strike and dost heal,
and thy blessing is holy and pure, let thy saints bless thee, and
all the creatures of thine hand, and let thine angels praise thee
for ever, and blessed be thy glorious name, for thou hast given
us joy with thy great bounty, and not as we suspected. Blessed
art thou, O God, because thou hast had pity on them both,
grant them peace and mercy and joy in their lives for ever.
Then his servants came, and he said to them, Cover the grave
before any man perceive it. And he said to his wife, Prepare
me much meat, and run to the flock, and take thence calves and
sheep, and command that a good feast be made, and she did so.
And he said to Tobiyyah, Thou shalt not depart from my house
before fourteen days, but make joyful my forsaken daughter, and
take half of my goods now, and when I and my wife are dead,
thou shalt take all ; thou shalt be to me a dear son, and I will
be to thee a father, and Ednah my wife a mother for ever.

CHAPTER IX.

Then Tobiyyah called Raphael, and said to him, My brother
Azaryah, take with thee hence four servants and two camels,
and go to Rages to Gabael, and give him his bag, and he will
give thee the money, and invite him to my wedding, for I cannot
go thither, since Reuel hath sworn that I shall not depart from
his house before fourteen days. But my father counteth the days,
and if one day exceed the time my father's soul will be grieved,
and I cannot make void the oath of Reuel. Raphael went with
two camels and four servants to the city Rages, and they lodged

in the house of Gabael, and [Raphael] gave him his bag, and told
him that Tobiyyah, the son of Tobi, was married to Sarah, the
daughter of Reuel, and that Tobiyyah had invited him to come to
his wedding. When Gabael heard that, he laded the camels
with the money, and came to the wedding. And he found Tobiyyah sitting at the table, and he kissed him, and wept on him
from exceeding joy, and blessed him, saying, The God of heaven
bless a good and honest man, who giveth much alms; and blessed
be the God of my kinsman Tobi, who hath given thee and thy
father and thy mother this good wife.

CHAPTER X.

Now Tobi counted every day the days of his son, how many
days he needed to go to receive the money, and how many days
to return. And when the days according to his reckoning were
expired, and Tobiyyah his son came not back, he said to himself,
They perhaps detain him there, or Gabael is dead, and they gave
him not the money. And he began to be uneasy. Then his
wife Hannah said to him, My son has perished, and his soul is
not alive, and therefore is he behind time. And she began to
mourn and weep for her son, saying, Woe is me, my son, that
I sent thee to go to a distant land; the light of mine eyes, why
did I let thee go? And Tobi said to her, Be silent, be not afraid,
thy son will arrive in peace. He has met only with an accident,
and the man who went with him is truthful. Be not troubled, for
he will arrive in peace. But Hannah said to him, Be silent, and
comfort me not concerning my son. And she went out into the
crossway by day and by night to the place where her son should
arrive, and she ate nothing but tears in the night, and her heart
had no rest. And when the fourteen wedding-days were expired,
Tobiyyah said to Reuel, Let me go, for my father and mother
look no more to see me, so now, I pray thee, let me go, for
I can no longer stay. Reuel said to him, Tarry with me yet
awhile, and I will send to declare to thy father all that thou
hast done. Tobiyyah answered him, Give me leave to return to

my father. Then Reuel arose and gave Sarah his daughter to Tobiyyah, and half his goods, servants, and asses, and camels, sheep, and oxen, and garments, and vessels of silver and gold, and he sent them away in tranquillity and quietness. And he blessed them, saying to them, God give you peace, and grant that I may see children of you before I die. And he embraced them, and kissed them, and said to his daughter Sarah, Take heed to honour thy father and thy mother-in-law, which are both thy parents. Go in peace, and may I hear good report of thee and great joy. And he kissed her and sent her away. And Ednah said to Tobiyyah, Thou art my son and my brother, may the God of heaven lead thee in peace, and let me see righteous children before me of Sarah my daughter. Now, behold, Sarah my daughter is in thy hand, entreat her not evil all the days of her life. Go in peace. I am thy mother, and Sarah is thy wife. May God prosper your ways all the days of your lives. And she kissed them and sent them away. And Tobiyyah went away joyful, and blessed the God of heaven and earth, who had sent his angel and prospered his journey, and blessed Reuel and Ednah his wife, saying, May God help me to honour you all the days of your lives.

CHAPTER XI.

And Tobiyyah went on till he came to the city Akris, which is over against Nineveh. Raphael said to Tobiyyah, My brother, thou knowest how thou didst leave thy father. Now therefore let thy wife go behind us with our men, and I and thou will go to prepare the house. So they went both of them first. And they found his mother sitting on the crossway looking about for her son. And when she saw him, she ran to meet him. And she embraced and kissed him, saying, Blessed be God, who hath brought thee back in peace, for I counted to see thy face never more. And now, my son, why didst thou delay to come? And he told her everything. And she was exceeding glad, and said to him, Go thou to thy father, and I will stay here until thy wife cometh.

d

So Tobiyyah went, and Raphael with him. And when Tobi heard that his son was come, he was exceeding glad, and said to him, My son, come towards me that I may kiss thee, for I cannot go towards thee. Then Raphael said to Tobiyyah, Take the gall of the fish and put it on his eyes. And God made his eyes whole as they were before. And Tobi rejoiced at the great goodness which God had shown him. And Tobi blessed God, saying, Blessed be God, who hath not withholden his bounty from me, and hath brought me out of darkness to light. It is thou who strikest and healest. There is none like thee, who healeth for no reward, and there is no god in heaven or on earth who doeth mighty deeds like thine. Tobiyyah then related to his father all that he had done. And they prepared the house. Then Tobi went forth with his son Tobiyyah to meet his daughter-in-law, and Raphael with them. And it came to pass, when he saw her, that he rejoiced over her, and brought her into his house, and blessed her, saying, May God give thee of this wife righteous children, and may mine eyes and the eyes of thy mother behold them.

Chapter XII.

Now when they went into the house, Raphael did not enter with them, but went his way. After a time Tobi said to Tobiyyah, Go out into the market-place, and call our brother Azaryah, that I may give him his wages, and we will add to them, because he is a trusty and honest man. And Tobiyyah went out into the market-place, and sought, but found not Raphael, and he enquired about him of all the people of the town, but he did not find a man who had seen him. He returned to his father, and said to him, I have found him not. Then his father knew that it was the angel Raphael, whom God had sent to deliver Sarah from the hands of the demon, and to heal his eyes. And he blessed God, saying, Blessed be God, who sent his good angel with my son, and who prospered his journey, and hath healed two poor and sick people like ourselves. And from that day forward God prospered Tobi and Tobiyyah his son, and gave him children of his wife Sarah. And Reuel and Ednah his wife died, and Tobiyyah inherited all their goods.

After days Tobi fell sick, and called his son Tobiyyah, and enjoined him the commandments of God, saying to him, My son, do goodness all thy days to the poor and the rich, and give alms all thy days, for the sake of which God will bless all the works of thine hands. The Lord blessed Abraham our father on account of the alms and tithes which he gave; and also Isaac for that he gave tithe and did almsdeeds; and so when Jacob went to the house of Laban and prayed, he vowed only to give tithe [and] alms to the poor, and therefore God made him prosperous, and gave him all that he asked, and preserved him from Laban and his brother Esau. And if thou do like as they did, he will bless thee as he blessed them. And he enjoined them other commandments, and when he had made an end of doing so, he was gathered to his people. And Tobiyyah his son buried him with great honour. And after his death God blessed Tobiyyah, because he fulfilled the commandments of his father, and he made him exceeding prosperous, and bestowed blessing on all the works of his hands.

Behold we learn how great is the power of alms and tithes. Because Tobi gave alms and separated his tithes, as is meet, how the Holy One (blessed is he) rewarded him! And because the fathers of the world knew the power of alms, therefore they gave heed to them. Of Abraham it is written, 'And he gave him tithes of all' (Gen. xiv. 20); of Isaac it is written, 'Then Isaac sowed in that land' (Gen. xxvi. 12), and 'sowing' means nothing else than alms, as it is said, 'Sow to yourselves in alms' (Hos. x. 12); of Jacob it is written, 'And of all that thou shalt give me I will surely give the tenth unto thee' (Gen. xxviii. 22).

THE END OF THE HISTORY OF TOBIYYAH.

PRAISE TO GOD!

II. TRANSLATION OF THE HEBREW.

BOOK OF TOBIT.

CHAPTER I.

THIS is the book of Tobi, the son of Tobiel, the son of Hananel, the son of Ariel, the son of Gabael, the son of Asael, the son of Nenathiel, of the tribe of Naphthali, who was led captive from Samaria with the captivity which was taken away in the days of Hoshea, the son of Elah, who was led captive in the days of Shalmaneser, king of Assyria. And he was of the inhabitants of a city of Naphthali, which is in Galilee, on the western boundary. And Tobi said, Remember me, my God, for good, forasmuch as I have walked before thee all the days of my life in an upright way, and for the many almsdeeds and great kindnesses which I have done to my brethren and my nation in the captivity at Nineveh in the land of Assyria. And it came to pass when I was but young in the land of Israel, that all the tribe of Naphthali rebelled against the house of David, and refused to go to Jerusalem, the city which the Lord chose out of all the tribes of Israel, wherein was the altar of the Lord that was sanctified for all the tribes of Israel, and the temple of the Lord was built in the midst thereof for offering up the burnt-offerings and the thank-offerings to the Lord three times a year. And all the brethren of the tribe of Naphthali offered sacrifices and burnt-offerings to the golden calves, which Jeroboam, the son of Nebat, king of Israel, had made in Bethel and Dan. But I went to Jerusalem at the feasts, according as it is written in the law of the Lord for Israel, with the firstfruits and the tithes and the firstlings for the priests, the sons of Aaron; and corn and new wine and oil and figs and pomegranates and of every fruit of the land for the sons of Levi that ministered before the Lord in Jerusalem; and the second tithe and the third tithe for the stranger, the orphan, and the widow; and I went every year with all these things to Jerusalem, according to the commandment of the Lord, and as Deborah, my father's mother, commanded me, for I was left an orphan by my father and my mother. And when I grew up, I took a wife of my family, whose name was Hannah, and she bare me a son, and I called his name Tobiyyah. Now when I was carried captive from the land of Naphthali, I dwelt in Nineveh the great city, and all my brethren and kinsmen did eat the bread of the Gentiles, but I defiled myself not with their dainties, because I feared the Lord, and remembered the Lord with all my heart and with all my soul. So God gave me grace and favour in the eyes of Shalmaneser, king of Assyria, and he appointed me over all that he had unto the day of his death. And I committed to the hand of my brother Gabael, who was in the land of Media, at the city Rages, ten talents of silver. And it came to pass, when Shalmaneser, king of Assyria, died, that Sennacherib his son reigned in his stead, and the highways of Media were closed because of the wars which were in the land, and I could not go to the land of Media to receive my money. And after this I gave many alms to the poor of my nation, who were orphans and widows, and when I saw the slain of my nation cast forth outside the wall of Nineveh, I kept not quiet, and rested not until I had buried them. Now it came to pass, when Sennacherib, king of Assyria, returned from Judah to Nineveh with confusion of face, because that the Lord God of Israel had smitten him in the land of Judah for the reproach wherewith he reproached and blasphemed the God of Israel, that therefore he was wroth with all the congregations of Israel throughout his kingdom, and he killed exceeding many of them. And I sought to know the truth of the matter, why this calamity came upon the tribe of Israel, for I know of a truth that the Holy One (blessed is he) is a God of truth and without iniquity, and I found that the tribes of Israel did not lay to heart the destruction of their brethren, which Sennacherib, king of Assyria, had brought on them; their strongholds he set on fire, and their young men he slew with the sword, and their women with-child he ripped up. For instead of mourning and afflicting themselves before the Lord concerning the persecution of their brethren, and because that he was wroth with them, they were eating and drinking and making merry, delighting themselves with instruments of song and harps and psalteries, and were not grieved for the destruction of Judah for our wickednesses and the wickednesses of our fathers, as it is written concerning Judah, 'That drink wine in bowls, and anoint themselves with the chief ointments; but they are not grieved for the affliction of Joseph.' Even for this was wrath from the Lord upon Judah and Jerusalem, and he brought against them the king of Babylon, until he cast them out from his presence, and he carried Judah away from his land. And when I saw the slain of Israel cast forth outside the wall, I many times stole their corpses and buried them, and I said, O Lord God of Israel, thou art righteous in all that hath come upon us, for thou hast dealt truly, and we have done wickedly. And when Sennacherib, king of Assyria, sought the slain of my nation, the corpses of the men who were killed, and found them not; then went the men of Nineveh and told the king, saying, Thy servant Tobi, whom thou hast appointed over all that thou hast, he sendeth his men over all the streets of Nineveh to seek the slain of his nation, and he burieth them privily, and feareth thee not. And it came to pass when Sennacherib heard this, that his anger was greatly kindled against me, and he commanded them to seize me, and Hannah my wife, and Tobiyyah my son, and he sought to slay me in his wrath, and when this matter was known to me I fled from his presence; and he commanded them to spoil all that I had, and I hid from his presence, until that the

widows and orphans of Israel cried out for me in the bitterness of their soul with fasting and weeping, and his judgment
reached unto heaven, and was lifted up even to the skies, and the
God of Israel delivered him into the hand of his two sons, and they
slew him with the sword. For he asked his counsellors and his
elders why the Holy One (blessed is he) had been jealous for Israel
and Jerusalem, and the angel of the Lord destroyed the host of
Pharaoh and all the firstborn of Egypt, and the young men by
whose hand the Lord always gave them salvation. And his
wise men and his counsellors said to him, Abraham, the father
of Israel, led forth his son to slay him, peradventure he might
thereby obtain the favour of the Lord his God; therefore hath
he been jealous for his children, and hath executed vengeance
upon thy servants. Then the king said, I will slay my two
sons for the Lord's sake, peradventure I may obtain by them
God's favour, and he will help me. And the saying came to
Adrammelech and Sharezer his sons, and they laid in wait for
him, and killed him with the sword, at the hour when he went
in to pray before his idol Dagon, as it is said, 'And Adrammelech and Sharezer his sons smote him with the sword, and they
escaped into the land of Ararat.' And it came to pass when
Sennacherib, king of Assyria, was dead, that Esarhaddon his
son reigned in his stead. And Esarhaddon appointed Akikar,
the son of my brother Hananel, over all that he had, and he
ruled over all the land of Assyria. And Akikar spake kind
words for me to the king, so that he brought me back to
Nineveh, for Akikar was my friend and kinsman. And they
restored me my wife Hannah and my son Tobiyyah, for the
king of Assyria had commanded them to be seized in his rage
against me.

CHAPTER II.

Now the same year at the feast of weeks I prepared in my
house a great feast, and I sat at my table to eat. Then I said
to my son Tobiyyah, Go and bring one of our poor brethren to

eat with us, and I and all who sit with me will not eat until
thou comest. So my son Tobiyyah went to seek of the poor,
and he returned in bitterness of soul, and said to me, My father,
one of our brethren hath been slain, and cast out in the street
of the city. And when I heard it I was troubled and in sore
distress, and I left my table, and went, and lifted him up from
the street, and took him in my keeping until the going down of
the sun, that I might be able to bury him. Then I returned to
my house, and ate my bread with tears and lamentation, and
I remembered the word which the prophet Amos uttered in
Bethel, saying, 'And I will turn your feasts into mourning,' etc.
And I wept very sore. And it came to pass when the sun
went down, that I went and buried him that was slain. But
my kinsmen and my family mocked me, saying, This man feareth
not for his soul, and he burieth the slain! And on that night
after I had buried him who was dead I washed, but was not
able to purify myself in an unclean land, as it would have been
meet in the land of Israel, according as the prophet Jeremiah
said of us, 'Thou shalt not be made clean any more.' Then
I went and laid down by the wall, and my face was uncovered,
and I knew not that there were birds above me on the wall. And
their dung fell upon mine eyes, and there came a whiteness in
mine eyes. And I went in the morning to the physicians to
heal me, but they could not, and I was blind four years. And
all my brethren and kindred were grieved at my blindness, and
Akikar my kinsman did nourish me. Now at that time my
wife Hannah did work for women, and weaved curtains for
others, and received her wages. And there was a day when
they gave her a kid for her wages. And I heard the voice of
the kid crying out. Then I said to her, Whence cometh this
kid? Beware lest it be stolen. And she said to me, It is not
so, but it hath been given to me for my wages. But I did not
believe her, and exclaimed against her, saying, Go and restore
it to its owner. And we quarrelled together concerning the
matter of the kid. And Hannah answered and said to me,

Where are thy kindnesses and thine alms, which profit thee
not in the day of thy trouble? but thy reproach is known to
all the world.

CHAPTER III.

And I was grieved, and fainted, and was sick at my affliction,
and prayed before the Lord, and said, Righteous art thou,
O Lord, and thy judgment is upright, for all thy works are
might, and all thy ways are kindness and truth, and thou art
the judge of the earth, and thou art righteous in all that cometh
upon me, for thou hast dealt truly, and I have done wickedly.
Now therefore, O Lord, father of mercy, Lord of forgiveness,
remember me, I pray, and visit me after thy mercy and kindness, and reward me not according to my sin and wickedness,
and according to the wickedness of my fathers, who kept not
thy commandments, but cast thy law behind their back, so that
thou hast given us to be a reproach, a proverb, and a by-word
among all the nations, and that the nations should mock us,
amongst whom thou hast cast us out, as it is this day; and
except the Lord of hosts had left unto us a very small remnant,
we should have been as Sodom, and we should have been like
unto Gomorrah. Now therefore, O Lord, thy judgments are
many and true, reward me not after my wickedness and the
wickedness of my fathers, for we have sinned before thee, and
have not walked in thy ways. Now therefore deal with me
according as it is good and right in thine eyes, and take my
soul from me, for it is better for me to die than live, and I shall
no more hear my reproach. And on that same day it happened
to Sarah, the daughter of Reuel, who lived at Agbatanis, a city in
the land of Media, that her father's maidservants were reproach-
ing her and mocking her, saying to her, It is not meet to call
thee Sarah, but Zarah [trouble]. For she had been given to wife
to seven husbands, and not one of them had approached her,
but Asmodeus, the king of the demons, had killed them before
they approached her after the way of all the earth. And the

maid said to her, Why dost thou kill thine husbands, and
beat us because of this evil matter? It would be good for
thy parents that thou shouldest die for them, and that they see
not of thee either son or daughter for ever. And it came to
pass when Sarah heard this reproach, that she was grieved sore.
And she wept, and went up to her father's upper chamber, and
cried before the Lord with a bitter voice, and said, O Lord God,
thou hast given me to my parents, who are old and well
stricken in age, and thou hast sent against my husbands that
married me the king of the demons, for thou art the God of all
the spirits and all the demons, and the maker of all creatures,
and in thy hand are all the kinds of evil spirits which are in the
world. Now therefore, O Lord, is it good in thine eyes that
I should bring down the old age of my father and my mother
in sorrow to the grave? for if the sentence of judgment hath
gone forth from before thee against me in this matter, destroy
me utterly, I pray, and let me see no longer my exceeding trouble
and my great reproach. Thou knowest, O Lord, that I am pure
from all pollution with man, and that I have not polluted my
name nor the name of my parents in the land of my captivity.
And I am the only child of my father and my mother, neither
hath he son to possess his inheritance, nor hath he a kinsman
who may possess me. And behold seven husbands are dead for
my sake, and what profit have I in being any longer in the
world? But if it be not good in thine eyes to kill me, look and
answer me, and have mercy on me, that I may hear my reproach
no more. At that time the prayer of them both was heard before
the throne of glory, the prayer of Tobi concerning his blindness, and the prayer of Sarah concerning the humiliation of her
parents. And the Lord sent the angel Raphael, the prince
who is appointed over healing, to heal them twain, to heal
Tobi, the father of Tobiyyah, of the disease in his eyes, and to
give Sarah, the daughter of Reuel, to Tobiyyah, the son of Tobi,
to wife, and to take away from her Asmodeus, the king of the
demons.

CHAPTER IV.

And when Tobi had finished his prayer he returned to his house. And Sarah, the daughter of Reuel, came down from her father's upper chamber, when she had made an end of praying to the Lord. At that time Tobi remembered the money which he had committed to the hand of Gabael in the city Rages in the land of Media. And he said in his heart, Behold I ask every day to die; now therefore I will call my son Tobiyyah, and will signify him of the matter of the money before I die. So Tobi called his son, and said to him, When I am dead, bury me with honour, and honour thy mother, and forsake her not all the days of her life, and oppose not her desire. And make not her life bitter, for remember, my son, what troubles passed over her when thou wast in her womb; and when she is dead, bury her by me with honour in one grave. And remember thy Creator all thy days, and sin not before him, and transgress not his commandments. And withhold not thy hand from giving alms of all which the Lord giveth thee, and keep not company with violent men. Hide not thine eyes from the poor of Israel, so shall the Lord not hide his eyes from thee in the time of thy trouble. And if thou art not able to make riches, cease not to give alms of that which is found in thine hand, so shalt thou acquire for thyself riches and treasures of silver and gold by almsgiving, for the treasures of the wicked shall not profit, and alms doth deliver from death; and every one who occupieth himself in alms shall behold the face of God, as it is written, 'I will behold thy face by almsgiving,' and in heaven they pay special regard to him. And thou, my son, withdraw thyself from all uncleanness and from all whoredom, and take thee a wife of thy family, and not of any stranger, which is not of the seed of thy fathers, for we are of the sons of the prophets. And remember, my son, Abraham, Isaac, and Jacob, who took wives of their own family, and would not make marriages with the strangers, and they were blessed with sons and daughters, And thou, my son, give thine heart to all thy work, and that which thou hatest to be done to thee, do not thou to others. And let not the wages of him that is hired abide with thee all night on the day when thou dost agree with him, and thy work God will repay thee. And withdraw thyself from drunkenness, and there shall no evil happen unto thee. And give of thy bread to the hungry, and with thy garments cover the naked, and of all which remaineth over give alms, and let it not be hard in thine eyes. Spend freely thy bread and wine on the burial of the righteous, and hearken and attend to every one who giveth thee good counsel. And at all times ask of the Lord, and he shall direct thy paths and thy counsel, for there is no counsel in the power of man, but in the hands of the Holy One (blessed is he) alone, for he doeth whatsoever pleaseth him, one he bringeth low, and another he lifteth up. And keep my words, and all that I have commanded thee, and let them not depart from thine eyes. And be strong and of good courage, for the Lord will be with thee a help and profit, if thou seek him with all thy heart and all thy soul. And now, my son, I will signify to thee the matter of the money which I have in the hand of Gabael my brother and kinsman, ten talents of silver in the city Rages in the land of Media, for I know not the day of my death. And thou, my son, if thou fear the Lord and keep thyself from all sin, he will give thee great riches.

CHAPTER V.

Then Tobiyyah answered his father and said, All that thou hast commanded me, my father, I will do. Now therefore, my father, give me counsel how I can receive the money from the hand of Gabael, for he will not know me, and I shall not know him; and what sign shall I give him so that he may give me the money? and I know not either the ways by which they go to Media. Then Tobi answered and said to Tobiyyah, This is the sign that thou shalt give him. He gave me his bag, and

took from my hand mine, when I put the money in his hand
this day twenty years ago. Now therefore go and seek thee a
man who may be trusty to go with thee, and we will give him
his wages; and go, my son, while I yet live, and receive the
money, and may the Lord God of Israel keep thee in all thy
journey, and grant thee favour, kindness, and mercy in the man's
eyes, and in the eyes of all that see thee, and may he send thee
away in honour and peace, and bring thee back to us in peace
before I die. So Tobiyyah went forth to seek a man to go with
him to Media, and he found Raphael, an angel of the Lord,
standing over against him, but Tobiyyah knew not that he was
an angel of the Lord of hosts. Then the angel said to Tobiyyah,
From whence art thou, young man? And Tobiyyah answered
and said, I am of the children of Israel. Then Tobiyyah said,
My lord, knowest thou how to go with me to Media? And the
angel said, Yea, I know all the ways, and in Media I have been
a guest in the house of our brother Gabael, who dwelleth at
Rages, a city of Media, and it is a two days' journey from Agbatanis to Rages, and Rages is built on a mountain, but Agbatanis
is built on the plain. Then Tobiyyah said to him, Stay of thy
kindness a moment, and I will go and declare the matter to my
father, for I desire greatly that thou shouldest go with me, and
I will give thee the wages of the journey. And he said to him,
Go in haste, for behold I wait until thou comest back to me,
and tarry not. Then Tobiyyah came and told his father, saying,
I have found a good man of our brethren to go with me. And
Tobi said, Call him to me, that I may know of what place he is,
and whether he be trusty to go with thee. So Tobiyyah went
forth and called him. And the angel came to Tobi, and said to
him, Peace be unto thee, thou man of God. But Tobi said, If
it is peace to me, why then hath all this befallen me, for I see
not with mine eyes, but I sit blind in darkness? Then the angel
said, He who hath deprived thee of light, the same shall heal
thee, for thou art a righteous man. And Tobi answered and
said, Let the Lord say so. Then Tobi said to him, My brother,

my son Tobiyyah seeketh to go to Media, canst thou go to Media?
canst thou go with him, and I will give thy wages? And the
angel said, Yea, I can, for I know all the ways, and have tra-
versed all the boundaries, and know the mountains. Then Tobi
said, Of what place art thou, and of what tribe art thou, and of
what city art thou? And the angel said, Dost thou still enquire,
when thou hast a hired man to go with thy son according to thy
wish? Then Tobi said, My brother, I wish to know thy name,
and of what family thou art. And the angel said, I am Azaryah,
the son of Hananel, of the family of the great Shelomith, of thy
brethren. Then Tobi said, Life and peace to thee! Now therefore, my brother, be not provoked with me for that I enquire
to know the matter of the ancestors of thy family, for, behold, my
brother, thou art of a good and honourable family, and also
thou knowest Hananel and Nathan, the two sons of the great
Shelomith, and it was they who went with me to Jerusalem, when
we dwelt in the land of Israel, and worshipped with me there,
and these did not stray after the strange gods of the land, like
our brethren. Now therefore, my brother, go in peace with my
son, and come ye back in peace with the help of God, and I will
give thy wages, a drachm every day, and thy food as for my son,
and, if the Holy One (blessed is he) bring you back in peace, I
will yet add to thy wages. And the angel said, Fear not, for
I will go with thy son, and we shall go in peace, and we shall
return in peace. Then Tobi called his son, and said to him,
Prepare thee what thou needest for the journey, and go with
thy brother, and may God Almighty lead you in peace, and bring
you back in peace, and send his angel with you, and prosper
your journey. And Tobiyyah kissed his father and his mother,
and they said to him, Go in peace. And they set out to go.
Then his mother began to weep, and said to her husband, How
didst thou not fear to send away the young man, for he is the
son of our old age, who goeth out and cometh in before us?
And without that money our God will keep us alive. And
Tobi said to her, Fear not, my sister, for he will go in peace and

will come back to us in peace, and thine eyes shall see him.
And the Lord our God will send his angel with him, and will
prosper his journey, and he will return in peace. But she
wept yet more.

CHAPTER VI.

So the young man went on his way, and the angel Raphael
with him. And he came in the evening to the river Tigris, and
they passed the night there. And Tobiyyah went down to the
river to wash his feet. And a fish came suddenly out of the
river, and devoured the young man's bread. And he cried out.
Then the angel said to him, Lay hold of the fish, and do not
let it go. So the youth laid hold of the fish. Then the angel
said to the young man, Open the fish in the middle, and take
the heart and the gall, and put them by thee, for they are good
for healing. And the young man did so. And he cooked the
fish, and ate, and the remainder he left. And they went on till
they came to Media. Then Tobiyyah said to the angel, My
brother Azaryah, what healing wilt thou perform with the heart
and gall of the fish? And he said to him, The heart is good
to smoke thereof before a man in whom is an evil spirit or
the spirit of demons, and it will flee from him. And the gall
is good for anointing therewith the eyes in which is whiteness,
and they will be healed. And they came to Agbatanis, and the
angel said to Tobiyyah, My brother, we shall pass the night in
the house of Reuel, for he is an old man, and hath an only
daughter, fair of form, whose name is Sarah, and I will speak to
him that he may give her to thee to wife. And she is of good
understanding, and her father loveth her. Now therefore hear
me, and speak for her, and when we shall return from Rages, we
will celebrate the marriage. For I know that the man will not
oppose thy desire, and that he will not give her to a stranger, but
thou shalt marry her, according to the law of Moses, and we
shall lead her to thy father. Then Tobiyyah said to the angel, I
have heard, my brother, that she hath already been given to

seven husbands, who died before they came in unto her, and I have heard that Asmodeus, the king of the demons, killed them. Now therefore I am greatly afraid lest Asmodeus kill me, and I bring the old age of my parents in sorrow to the grave, for they have no other son, neither daughter, to bury them when they die. Then the angel said to him, Fear the Lord, and remember him, and remember the commandments of thy father which he commanded thee, that thou shouldest take a wife of the family of thy father. Now therefore hear me, and be not afraid of the demon. For I know that thou shalt take her this night to wife. And when thou shalt enter the chamber with her, take the heart of the fish, and smoke thereof under her garments, and the demon shall smell it, and flee, and return to her no more. And when thou shalt desire to approach her, rise ye from the bed, and pray, and supplicate the Lord that he would command his kindness and healing upon you, and heal her. And then thou shalt approach her, and shalt beget of her sons ; and fear not, for for thee was she meet before the world was created, and by thine hand the Lord shall save her from the hand of the demon.

CHAPTER VII.

And it came to pass when Tobiyyah heard all these sayings, that his soul was knit to the soul of Sarah. And they came to Agbatanis to the house of Reuel, and found him by the door of his house, and they saluted him. And he saluted them again. And he said to them, Go into the house in peace. And they went into the house. Then Reuel said to Ednah his wife, How like is this youth to Tobi my brother ! And Ednah asked them, My brethren, whence are ye ? And they answered her, Of the captivity, which is in Nineveh, of the tribe of Naphthali. Then she said to them, Know ye our brother Tobi ? And they said, We know him. Then she said to them, Is he well ? And they said, He is well. Then Tobiyyah said, Your brother Tobi, of whom ye speak, is my father. And Reuel ran to meet him, and embraced him, and kissed him, and wept with him.

And Reuel said, Blessed art thou, my son, of the Lord, for thou
art the son of a righteous and upright man. And Reuel and
Ednah his wife and Sarah his daughter wept yet more with him.
And he killed a ram, and they prepared a feast with a glad
heart; and they ate and drank. Then Tobiyyah said to the
angel, Speak with Reuel concerning the matter of Sarah his
daughter, that he give her to me to wife. And it came to pass
when Reuel heard this matter, he said to Tobiyyah, I know, my
son, that it is better that I give her to thee than that I give her
to another husband, but I will tell thee the truth. My son,
know that I have already given her to seven husbands, who all
died before they came in unto her. But now eat and drink, and
leave the matter alone. But Tobiyyah said, I will neither eat
nor drink before thou hast given her to me to wife. Then
Reuel said, Take her, for she is thy sister, and thou art her
brother. Behold, I give her to thee to wife, according to the
law of Moses and Israel, and may the Lord God of heaven
make you dwell this night in peace, and command upon you his
kindness and his peace. Then Reuel took Sarah his daughter,
and gave her to Tobiyyah to wife, and he blessed them, and
bade Ednah his wife bring him a tablet, and he wrote thereon
the deed of marriage, and he sealed it before witnesses. And
they ate and drank and were merry. And Reuel said to Ednah
his wife, Prepare the chamber, and put them therein. And
Ednah embraced Sarah her daughter, and wept with her, and
said to her, My daughter, may the Lord God of Israel shew thee
kindness this night, and grant thee mercy, and have pity on
thee because of the sorrow which hath passed over thee unto
this day.

CHAPTER VIII.

And it came to pass when they had finished preparing the
chamber and the bed, that Tobiyyah and Sarah arose and went
to the chamber. And Tobiyyah remembered the words of Raphael, and took the heart of the fish, and put it upon the pan,

and smoked under Sarah's garments. And Asmodeus received
the smell, and went out thereat, and fled to the end of the land
of Egypt, and the angel Raphael bound him there. And he
went out of the chamber and they shut the door on them twain.
Then Tobiyyah rose from the bed, and said to Sarah his wife,
My sister, arise, and let us present our supplication before God,
that he would deal with us after the abundance of his mercy
and kindness. And Tobiyyah entreated the face of the Lord,
and Tobiyyah said, O Lord God of Israel, thou art Lord alone
in heaven and on earth. And thou didst create Adam, and
gavest him Eve his wife for a helper like unto him. Now
therefore, O Lord, it is manifest and known to thee that I take
not this my sister for lust, but in uprightness of heart, according
to the law of Moses and Israel. And thou, O Lord, have mercy
upon us, and have compassion on us, and join us together in
peace, and give us sons who may be a blessing, occupying themselves in thy law. And Sarah answered and said, Amen. And
he went in unto her that night. Now Reuel arose in the night
and bade his servants dig a grave by night, saying, If the
youth is dead, we will bury him in the night, so that no man
know it, and there will be no reproach to us. And Reuel called
Ednah his wife, and said to her, Send one of the maids to the
chamber, that she may see whether he be alive; for if not, we
will bury him before the light of morning, and no man shall
know it. So Ednah sent the maid to the chamber, and she
looked, and behold they were both of them asleep together in
peace and joy. And she came forth and told them, and said to
them, He liveth. Then they blessed the Lord the great God ;
and Reuel said, Blessed art thou, O Lord God of our fathers,
who hast shewn us this great kindness, for it is thou, O Lord,
who smitest and healest, and killest and makest alive, who hast
wrought this wonder with these twain, and thou livest and art
established for ever and ever. Then Reuel said to his servants,
Cover the grave before the morning, so that no man know it.
And he bade them prepare a great feast with joy, for God had

made them glad with the abundance of his mercy and kindness. And Reuel ran to the flocks, and brought calves and rams, and bade them prepare them. And he said to Tobiyyah, Thou shalt not depart from my house before fourteen days, but gladden my forsaken daughter. And thou shalt take half of all that I have, and shalt go to thy father with joy, and when I and my wife be dead, thou shalt take the whole.

CHAPTER IX.

Then Tobiyyah called Raphael, and said to him, My brother Azaryah, take with thee hence four servants and two camels, and come, go to Rages, to Gabael my uncle, and give him his bag, and he will give thee the money; and invite him to come to my wedding, for I cannot go thither, because of the oath which Reuel hath sworn to me, that I shall not depart from his house before fourteen days. But my father and my mother count the days, and if one day exceed the time, I shall grieve my parents' soul. So Raphael arose, and took two camels and four servants, and went to Rages to the house of Gabael, and gave him his bag, and told him that Tobiyyah, the son of Tobi, was married to Sarah, the daughter of Reuel, and Raphael invited him to come to Tobiyyah's wedding. Then Gabael laded the camels with the money, and came to the wedding. And he found Tobiyyah sitting at the table, and embraced him, and kissed him, and wept with him from exceeding joy, and blessed him, saying, Blessed is the Lord God of Israel, who hath joined thee in joy to the woman, and may he in his mercy give thee sons by her, who occupy themselves in the law of the Lord.

CHAPTER X.

Now Tobi and his wife were counting the days and the nights, and sorrowing that they had sent him away, and weeping and afflicting themselves for him. And Tobi comforted Hannah his wife, saying, Be silent, for he will return in peace and in joy. But she refused to be comforted, and went out every day on the roads to see whether her son would come, and she tasted nothing but tears for days and nights. And it came to pass when the fourteen days of the wedding were expired, Tobiyyah said to Reuel, Let me go, for my father and my mother are counting the days, and they look no more to see me. But Reuel said, Tarry with me yet awhile, and I will send to declare to thy father all that thou hast done. And Tobiyyah said, Detain me not, let me go, that I may go to my father. Then Reuel gave Tobiyyah Sarah his daughter, and half his riches, and servants, and maidservants, and sheep, and cattle, and asses, and camels, and garments of fine linen and purple, and vessels of silver and gold, and he sent them away, and blessed them, saying, May God, the Lord God of our fathers, bless you, and let me see of you sons who occupy themselves in the law of the Lord. And he kissed them, and embraced them, and said to Sarah his daughter, Honour greatly thy father and thy mother-in-law, and go in peace, and may we hear while we live good report of thee with joy and gladness. And he kissed them, and embraced them, and let them go. And he said to Tobiyyah, My son, may the Lord God of heaven lead thee in peace, and let me see of thee and of Sarah my daughter children good in the sight of the Lord before I die. Behold now, Sarah my daughter is in thine hand, entreat her not evil all thy days; go ye in peace. So he blessed and kissed them, and sent them away.

CHAPTER XI.

And Tobiyyah went away rejoicing and ~~glad in heart~~. And he blessed the Lord, ~~who~~ had made him glad, and who had shewn him many wonders and great kindness. Then he went on, and came to the city Akris, which is over against Nineveh. And Raphael said, My brother Tobiyyah, thou knowest how thou didst leave thy father and thy mother. Now therefore I and thou will go first, and thy wife shall go behind us with the servants and our men. So they went on both of them. And Raphael said to Tobiyyah, Take with thee of the gall of the fish. And he took

it. And behold his mother, was sitting on the highway to see
whether her son would come. And she saw him afar off and
knew him, and said to Tobi her husband, Behold, my son
Tobiyyah cometh, and the man that went with him. Then
Raphael said to Tobiyyah, I know that thy father is blind, but
with this gall shall his eyes be opened, and he shall be healed.
And Hannah his mother ran to meet him, and she fell upon his
neck, and said, Now will I die, now that I have seen thy face.
And she wept on his neck yet more. And Tobi arose, and went
to meet his son, and he stumbled as he went, for he did not see.
And Tobiyyah ran to his father, and put the gall on his eyes,
and his eyes were cleared, and the whiteness fell from his eyes,
and he was healed. And he saw his son, and fell on his neck,
and said, Blessed is the Lord God of Israel, who openeth the
eyes of the blind, for he hath opened mine eyes. Blessed is he,
and blessed is his name for ever and ever, who hath shewn this
great kindness to me, for he smiteth and healeth, and killeth
and maketh alive; and blessed, yea, blessed is he who hath
prospered thy journey, and who hath brought thee back to us in
peace and quietness. Then Tobi went forth, and Hannah his
wife, to meet Sarah, the daughter of Reuel, their daughter-in-
law. And they rejoiced with her with great joy, and it seemed
an exceeding marvellous thing in the eyes of all that saw and
heard that Tobi's eyes were healed. And Tobi blessed Sarah his
daughter-in-law, saying, Blessed art thou, my daughter, of the
Lord, and blessed is the Lord, who hath brought thee to us with
joy. And they and all the Jews who were in Nineveh rejoiced
with great joy at this great kindness which the Lord had shewn
to Tobi and his son. And they gave Tobiyyah many precious
gifts.

CHAPTER XII.

Then Tobi said to Tobiyyah his son, My son, let us give the
man who went with thee his wages, and we will further add
thereto. And Tobiyyah said, My father, let us give him the
half of the silver which I have brought thence. For he led me

in peace, and hath brought me back in peace, and hath healed my wife, and hath obtained the money from the hand of Gabael, and hath healed thine eyes. What now ought we to give him for all this? So Tobiyyah called Raphael, and said to him, My brother Azaryah, come and take thy wages, half of the money which thou hast brought thence, for it is thy wages, and go in peace. Then Raphael said to Tobi and to Tobiyyah his son, Sing to the Lord a new song, and bless him, and sing praise to his name for all the goodness which he hath done unto you. And continue before him in prayer and supplication and alms all the days of your lives, for it is better in the sight of the Lord to give alms always than to heap up treasures of silver and gold. For alms doth deliver from death. And I will not hide from you any of the truth. Know that at the time when thou and Sarah thy daughter-in-law did pray and make supplication before the Holy One (blessed is he), on account of the tribulation of your soul, I offered your prayer before the throne of glory; and at the time when thou wast burying the dead I was with thee; and at the feast of weeks, when thou didst leave thy table, and go to bury the dead man, I was with thee. And God hath tried thee by the blindness of thine eyes, for the Lord trieth the righteous. And at the time of thy tribulation the Lord sent me to heal thee and Sarah thy daughter-in-law. Now I am the angel Raphael, one of the princes who minister before the throne of glory. And it came to pass when they heard all these sayings, they were sore afraid, and they fell on their faces. And Raphael said to them, Peace be unto you; fear not; bless the Lord for these great and wonderful things which he hath done unto you. Now as to myself, all the time I was with you ye saw me eat and drink, for so it appeared to your eyes, yet I did neither eat nor drink. Now therefore write you all these things in a book, and it shall be for a witness between you and your God all the days of your lives, and this thing shall be for a sign and a witness amongst all generations. And bless the Lord, and praise the remembrance of his holiness. And now let me go, and I will go to the God who sent me to you. So they sent him away, and blessed the Lord for all this. And the angel of the Lord went up to heaven, and appeared no more to Tobi and his son Tobiyyah.

CHAPTER XIII.

At that time Tobiyyah wrote down all these things with joy. And Tobi said, Blessed is the Lord the great God, who doeth marvellous things to his people and his servants. He smiteth and healeth, and killeth and maketh alive, and bringeth down to hell and lifteth up. Who hath dispersed us among the Gentiles; we are bound to publish all these marvellous works among the nations. And ye, O children of Israel, be strong, and let your heart be of good courage, and let not your hands be weak, for your work shall be rewarded, and he will wait that he may be gracious unto you, and will be exalted that he may have mercy upon you. For the Lord is a God of judgment; blessed are all they that wait for him. And ye, my children, continue in alms, prayer, and supplication before the lord of all the world, for alms and prayer drive back the decree, for it is said, ' And alms do deliver from death.' And blessed is the Lord, who hath shewn to me and my father and my forefathers, and every one who hath trusted in him, wonders, and marvels, and great and terrible things. O lord of the world, shew us in our days salvation and redemption by the coming of the Redeemer and the building of Ariel before the eyes of all Israel, as it is said, ' In his days Judah shall be saved and Israel shall dwell safely;' and it is written, ' And the ransomed of the Lord shall return;' and again, ' The Lord doth build up Jerusalem, he gathereth together the outcasts of Israel.' Blessed is the Lord for ever, Amen and Amen.

END OF THE BOOK OF TOBI, THE SON OF TOBIEL.
PRAISE TO GOD!

III. ADDITION TO THE MIDRASH THANḤUMÂ.

Section beginning 'Give ear' (Deut. xxxii. 1).

AND thus it is found in the book of R. Moses had-Darshan. 'He kept him as the apple of his eye' (Deut. xxxii. 10). The Holy One (blessed is he) keeps those whom he tries like a man who keeps the apple of his eye. We have an example in the following history. There was a certain man, rich, of high station, and learned in the oral law; the same had a daughter, of exceeding beauty, and moreover pious, who had been married three times to three men, but each time on the morning after the first night of her marriage they found her husband dead. She said, Men shall die for me no more, I will dwell in widow-hood and seclusion, until God shall look on me, and take compassion. And so she remained many days. Now that rich man had in another city a very poor brother, who had ten sons; and every day he and his eldest son brought in bundles of sticks from the wood, and sold them, and by this means he and his wife and children supported themselves. Once they did not sell any, and they had no money to buy bread, and that day they ate nothing. On the morrow it came to pass, when they went into the wood, that the father fainted away. The son's eyes ran with tears because of their poverty, and he lifted his eyes to heaven. The son considered in his heart, and, having taken leave of his father and mother, went to the city where his uncle dwelt. And when he entered his house, his uncle and likewise his wife and daughter were exceedingly

glad, and asked him after his father and his mother and the
children. He abode with him seven days, and at the end of
the seven days the young man went to his uncle, and said to
him, I have one request to ask of thee, deny me not. His uncle
said to him, Say, my son, what it is that thou desirest. He
replied, Swear to me. And so he did. Then he said, This is
the request that I ask of thee, give me thy daughter to wife.
When the man heard it he wept. Nay, my son, said he, nay,
for such is her way, unfortunately[1]. He replied, Even on these
terms. He said to him, If for the sake of my riches thou art
eager for her, marry her not, for I will give thee silver and
gold in abundance, for thou art a handsome and wise young man,
but take my advice, and endanger not thyself with her. He
answered, Thou hast already sworn concerning this matter.
The rich man saw how the matter stood, and consented. So he
went to his daughter, and told her what had passed between
them. When she heard this, she wept and cried out in the
bitterness of her soul, and lifted her eyes to heaven, and said,
Lord of the worlds, let thine hand be upon me, and let not all
these die for my sake. What did he do? He betrothed her,
and prepared a banquet, and invited the elders of the city, and
made a canopy, and the bridegroom sat inside it. And a certain
elder met him—it was Elijah of blessed memory—and he called
him out privately, and said to him, My son, I will give thee right
counsel, and depart not thou from my counsel. When thou
sittest down to eat, a poor man will come in unto thee clad in
black and tattered garments, barefooted, and his hair standing
up like nails[2], he is so poor that there is none like him in all the
world. When thou seest him, thou shalt arise from thy seat, and
seat him beside thee, and make him eat and drink; wait on him
with all thy ability, and pay him honour, and let not a word of
all which I have said to thee fall to the ground, so shalt thou

---

[1] Alluding to the death of her three husbands.
[2] Job iv. 15.

be left in peace; and now I go my way. So the old man went
away, and the bridegroom went in to his place. They sat down
to the banquet, and when they began to eat that poor man came
in, and when the bridegroom saw him he stood up from his
place, and behaved to him in every respect as the old man had
told him. After the banquet that poor man called the bridegroom, who took him to a chamber. He said to him, My son,
I am a messenger of God, and am come hither to take thy life.
He replied, My lord, give me time, a year or half a year. He
said, I will not do so. Then he said, If it be so, give me thirty
days or the seven days of the banquet. He said to him, I will
not give thee even a single day, for thy time is already come.
He replied, I pray thee, wait for me whilst I go and take
leave of my wife. In this respect, said he, I will agree to thy
request; go therefore and come back quickly. He went to
the chamber, where she was sitting alone and weeping and
praying to her Creator, and at the door of the chamber the
young man called out to her, and she came to open to him;
then she brought him into the chamber beside her, and caught
hold of him and kissed him. She said to him, My brother, why
art thou come? He answered, To take leave of thee, for
my time is come to depart after the way of all the earth, for
the angel is come, and hath informed me that he is come to
demand my life. She said, Thou shalt not go, but thou shalt
abide here, and I will go to him and speak with him. She
went, and found him, and asked him, Art thou the angel who
is come to demand my husband's life? He said to her, I am.
She replied, He shall not die now; it is written in the Law,
'When a man hath taken a new wife, he shall not go out to
war, neither shall he be charged with any business, but he shall
be free at home one year, and shall cheer up his wife which he
hath taken' (Deut. xxiv. 5); and the Holy One (blessed is he)
is truth, and his law is truth. Now if thou take his life thou
wilt make the law a lie; if thou accept my words, well; but if
not, thou shalt come with me to the great tribunal before the

Holy One (blessed is he). The Holy One (blessed is he) immediately rebuked the angel, and he went his way. That night the bride and bridegroom slept together; and the bride's father and her mother were weeping in their chamber; and when midnight came, the man and woman arose to prepare a grave for their son-in-law before the break of dawn. When they arose they heard the bride and bridegroom sporting and merry together; so they went into the room to see whether it were so; they saw, and were glad, and published it to the congregation, and gave praise to God. And this is an example how the Holy One (blessed is he) keeps those who trust in him.

IV. ITALA.

LIBER TOBIAE.

Caput I.

[1] LIBER sermonum Thobi, filii Thobiel, filii Ananihel, filii Gabahel, filii Asihel, filii Gadalel, filii Arabei, ex tribu Nepthalim; [2] qui captivus abductus est in diebus Salmannassar regis Assyriorum, ex Bihel civitate, quae est in dextera parte Edisse civitatis Nepthalim, in superioribus Galilaeae contra Naasson, post viam quae ducit in occidentem, ex sinistra parte Raphain. Ego Thobis in via veritatis ambulavi et justitiae, omnibus diebus vitae meae : [3] et eleemosynas feci multas fratribus meis, et nationi meae, et omnibus qui fuerunt mecum in captivitate, in terra Assyriorum in Ninive. [4] Et cum essem in terra mea Israel inter omnes junior, omnis tribus Nepthalim patris mei recessit de domo David, et ab Hierusalem civitate, quae est electa ex omnibus tribubus Israel, ubi altare constitutum est omnibus tribubus Israel, quod sanctificatum est in saecula. Tunc cum templum habitationis excelsi Dei aedificatum esset in Hierusalem, ut sacrificaret in ipso omnis progenies in aeternum, [5] et omnes fratres mei, omnisque domus Nepthalim patris mei, sacrificabant in Dan vitulo aureo, quem fecit Hieroboam rex Israel, et omnibus altissimis montibus Galilaeae : [6] ego autem solus ibam aliquoties in Hierusalem diebus festis, sicut scriptum est in toto Israel in praecepto sempiterno : primitias, et decimas armentorum et pecorum, et initia tonsurae pecorum meorum, haec habens mecum, dabam sacerdotibus filiis Aaron, et quod moris erat, de tritico, vino, et oleo, et ficu, malorum granatorum, et caeterorum pomorum

dividebam Levitis et servientibus.Domino, qui praesto erant
in Hierusalem; et secundam decimationem commutans in
pecunia sex annorum, ibam, et consummabam illam in Hierusalem, in loco sancto unoquoque anno : ⁷ et tertii ad decimationem ferebam proselytis, et orphanis, et viduis, faciens omnia
quae praecepta sunt in Israel; et dabam illis in tertio anno :
⁸ et manducabam illud secundum praeceptum quod scriptum est
de eis in lege Moysi, et sicut praecepit Debbora, mater patris
mei Thobihel, matri meae et patri meo, qui orfanum me reli-
quit, et mortuus est.   ⁹ Et postquam juvenis factus sum, accepi
uxorem nomine Annam ex natione mea, et genui ex illa filium,
et vocavi nomen ejus Thobiam.   ¹¹ Et postquam in captivitatem
deveni ad Assyrios in Niniven, ¹² et omnes fratres mei qui de
genere meo erant, manducabant de panibus gentium ; ego autem
custodivi animam meam, ut ne manducarem de escis illorum.
¹³ Et quoniam memor eram Dei in toto corde meo, dedit mihi
Dominus summus gratiam penes Salmannassar regem Assyriorum, ¹⁴ et comparabam illi omnia quaecunque volebat in usu
suo, ¹⁶ iens in regionem Mediam usque dum moriretur.   ¹⁷ Et
commendavi Gabelo fratri meo filio Gabahel, in Rages civitate
regionis Medorum, decem talenta argenti.   ¹⁸ Et postquam
mortuus est Salmannassar rex Assyriorum, regnavit Sennacherim filius ejus pro eo ; et viae terrae Medorum constantes
erant, et nemo poterat illuc ire postea.   ¹⁹ Et in diebus Salmannassar regis, multas eleemosynas feci omnibus de natione
mea, ²⁰ panem meum dividens esurientibus, et nudos vestiens ;
et qui projecti erant post murum Ninive ex natione mea mortui,
sepeliebam illos, ²¹ quos occidisset Sennacherim rex, de Judaea
fugiens propter defensionem quam fecit Dominus coeli de illo,
ob blasphemias illius ; multos enim filiorum Israel occidit in
ira sua.   Ego corpora illorum involvebam, et sepeliebam ; et
quaerebat illa rex, et non inveniebat.   ²² Et renuntiatum est
illi, quoniam ego sepeliebam illos, et quaerebat me occidere.
²³ Ego autem fugi, et direpta est omnis substantia mea ; et nihil
mihi remansit plus quam uxor mea Anna, et Thobias filius

meus. ²⁴ Et contigit dum laterem, post dies quadraginta quinque occiderunt regem illum duo filii sui, et fugerunt in montem Ararath. Et regnavit post eum Archedonassar filius ejus pro illo, et constituit Achicarum, filium fratris mei Anna-nihel, super omnem curam regni; et ipse habebat potestatem super omnem regionem. Tunc petiit Achicarus regem pro me, erat enim consobrinus meus; ²⁵ et descendi in Ninive in domum meam, et reddita est mihi uxor mea Anna, et filius meus Thobias.

Caput II.

¹ In Pentecosten die festo nostro, qui est sanctus a septem annis, et factum est mihi prandium bonum, et discubui ut pran-derem; et posita est mihi mensa, et vidi pulmentaria complura, ² et dixi Thobiae filio meo: Vade, et adduc quemcunque pau-perem inveneris ex fratribus nostris, qui sunt captivi in Ninive, qui tamen habet Deum in mente in toto corde suo; hunc adduc, ut manducet pariter nobiscum prandium hoc: ecce sustineo te, fili, donec venias. ³ Et abiit Thobias quaerere aliquem pauperem captivum ex fratribus nostris; et reversus, dixit mihi: Pater: et ego dixi: Quid est, fili? et ait mihi: Ecce unus ex fratribus nostris occisus laqueo circumdato, projectus jacet in publico. Et exsilivi, relicto prandio meo, antequam quicquam ex illo gus-tarem: ⁴ et sustuli illum de platea in domum apud me, donec sol occideret, ut illum sepelirem. ⁵ Et reversus, lavi, et man-ducavi prandium meum cum luctu, ⁶ et rememoratus sum ser-monum prophetae Amos, quod locutus est in Bethleem, dicens: Convertentur omnes dies festi vestri in luctum, et omnia cantica vestra in lamentationem: et lacrymatus sum. ⁷ Et postquam sol occidit abii, et fodi, et sepelivi eum. ⁸ Et omnes proximi mei deridebant me, dicentes: Quomodo non timet hic homo? jam enim inquisitus est hujus rei causa ut occideretur, et fugit, et perdidit substantiam suam, et iterum sepelire coepit mortuos. ⁹ Et iterum lavi ea hora, postquam sepelivi. ¹⁰ Et introivi in domum meam, et dormivi circa parietem, facie nuda propter

aestum; [11] et ignorabam quoniam passeres in pariete super me residebant, quorum stercora oculis meis calida et induxerunt albugines. Et ibam caecus ad medicos ut curarer, et quanto mihi medicamenta imponebant, tanto magis excaecabantur oculi mei maculis, donec perexcaecatus sum. Et eram inutilis oculis meis, annis quatuor. [15] Et omnes fratres et amici mei dolebant pro me: Achicarus autem pascebat me annis duobus, priusquam iret in Limaidam. [19] In illo tempore, Anna uxor mea deserviebat operibus mulierum, lanam faciens et telam, et ex mercedibus suis pascebat me: et mittebant, et adducebant illam ad texendum, et dabant ei mercedem suam. Septima autem die mensis Distri consummavit texturam, et reddidit dominis suis; et dederunt illi mercedem suam totam, [20] et insuper dederunt ei pro detexto, ad manducandum, hoedum de capris. [21] Et cum introisset ad me hoedus, coepit clamare; et vocavi ad me uxorem, et dixi illi: Unde est hic hoedus qui balat? vide, ne forte furtivus sit, redde illum dominis suis; nobis enim non licet manducare nihil furtivum. Et respondit mihi, et dixit: Munere mihi datus est supra mercedem. Et ego non credebam, sed magis dicebam illi: Furtivus est, redde illum dominis suis: et contendebam, et erubescebam coram illa, hujus rei causa. [22] Et irata est, quoniam non credebam illi; et respondens, dixit mihi: Ubi sunt justitiae tuae? [23] ecce quae pateris, omnibus nota sunt.

CAPUT III.

[1] Et contristatus animo, ingemui lacrymans; et introivi in atrium meum, et coepi orare cum gemitu animae meae, [2] et dixi: Justus es Domine, et omnia opera tua magna sunt, et omnes viae tuae misericordiae et veritatis plenae sunt, et judicium verum judicas in saecula. [3] Et nunc Domine memor esto mei, et respice in me: ne vindictam sumas de peccatis meis, et de negligentia mea, et parentum meorum qui peccaverunt ante te. [4] Quoniam non obedierunt praeceptis tuis, et tradidisti nos in direptionem, et captivitatem, et mortem, in exemplum, et fabulas, et improperium omnibus nationibus, in quibus nos dispersisti.

⁵ Et nunc, Domine, multa sunt judicia tua et vera, quae de me
exigas, et de peccatis meis, et parentum meorum, quia non
egimus secundum praecepta tua, non ambulavimus sinceriter
coram te. ⁶ Et nunc, Domine, secundum quod tibi placet fac
mecum, et praecipe recipi spiritum meum, ut jam dimittar desuper terra: quia expedit mihi mori magis quam vivere, quoniam
improperia falsa audio, et in magno sum taedio. Praecipe ergo,
Domine, ut dimittar ab hac necessitate, et da mihi refrigerium in
locum aeternum : et noli avertere a me faciem tuam, quia expedit mihi mori magis quam vivere, et pati tantam necessitatem
in vita mea, ne jam improperium audiam hominum. ⁷ Eadem
die contigit ut et Sarra filia Raguhelis, quae erat Exbatanis
civitate Medorum, ut et ipsa audiret improperium ab una ex
ancillis patris sui, ⁸ quoniam jam tradita erat viris septem, et
Asmodaeus daemonium nequissimum occidebat eos ea hora qua
ad illam introiebant ad concumbendum, sicut est solitum mulie-
ribus. ⁹ Et dixit illi ancilla sua : Tu es quae suffocas viros tuos;
ecce jam tradita es viris septem, et nullo eorum fruita es. Quid
nos flagellas, aut causa virorum tuorum, qui mortui sunt? vade
et tu cum illis, et nunquam ex te videamus filium neque filiam
in perpetuum. ¹⁰ Eadem hora contristata est anima puellae, et
lacrymans ascendit in locum superiorem patris sui, et voluit
laqueo vitam finire : et cogitavit : Ne forte improperent patri
meo, et dicant : Unicam habuisti filiam carissimam, et haec
collum sibi ligavit : et incipiam deducere senectutem patris mei
cum tristitia animi ad inferos; non est utile animam laqueo
fugare : ¹¹ at bonum est potius deprecari Dominum, ut moriar,
et jam nullum improperium audiam in vita mea, neque ego,
neque pater meus. ¹² Eodem tempore, exporrectis manibus ad
fenestram, deprecata est, ¹³ et dixit : Benedictus es Domine Deus
misericordiarum, et benedictum est nomen tuum sanctum, et
honorabile in omnia saecula. Benedicant tibi omnia opera tua
in aeternum. ¹⁴ Et nunc, Domine, ad te faciem meam levo, et
oculos meos dirigo. ¹⁵ Jube jam me dimitti desuper terra, ne
audiam improperia hominum. ¹⁶ Tu scis, Domine, quia munda

sum ab omni immunditia viri, et non coinquinavi corpus meum, neque dehonestavi nomen patris mei in terra captivitatis meae. Unica sum patri meo, et non habet alium filium, vel filiam, qui possideat haereditatem illius : neque frater est illi quisquam, vel proximus aut propinquus, ut custodiat me illi uxorem. Jam perierunt mihi viri septem; et quo mihi adhuc vivere? et si non tibi videtur, Domine, perdere me, aspice in me, et miserere mei, ut nullum jam improperium audiam. ²⁴ In illo tempore exauditae sunt preces amborum ab ipsa claritate summi Dei : ²⁵ et missus est Raphahel angelus sanare duos, id est, Thobin curare a maculis oculorum, et reddere ei aspectum luminis ; et Sarram filiam Raguhelis dare Thobiae filio Thobis uxorem, et colligare Asmodaeum daemonium nequissimum ab illa : quoniam Thobiae destinata erat haereditas ejus, super omnes qui illam concupierant. Uno igitur tempore reversus est Thobi de- atrio in domum suam, et Sarra filia Raguhelis descendit et ipsa de loco superiori.

Caput IV.

¹ Eadem die rememoratus est Thobis commendasse se pecu- niam Gabelo, in Rages civitate Medorum : et dixit in corde suo cogitans : Ecce ego postulavi mortem ; cur non voco Thobian filium meum, et indicabo illi de hac pecunia quam commendavi, antequam moriar? Et vocavit filium suum, ² et dixit illi : Fili : et ille respondit : Quid est, pater? Et Thobis dixit : ³ Fili, cum mortuus fuero, sepeli me diligenter : et honorem habe matri tuae, et noli derelinquere illam omnibus diebus vitae suae ; et quod illi placet, hoc fac in conspectu ejus, et noli contristari spi- ritum ejus in ulla re. ⁴ Memor esto, fili, quanta pericula passa sit pro te in utero suo : ⁵ et cum mortua fuerit, sepeli illam circa me in uno sepulcro. ⁶ Et omnibus diebus vitae tuae, fili, Deum in mente habe : et noli velle peccare, vel praeterire praecepta illius. Justitiam fac omnibus diebus vitae tuae, et noli ire in viam iniquitatis : quoniam, agente te ex veritate, erit respectus in operibus tuis, et omnibus qui faciunt justitiam. ⁷ Ex sub-

f

stantia tua, fili, fac eleemosynam, et noli avertere faciem tuam
ab ullo paupere : et ita fiet ut nec avertatur a te facies Dei.
⁸ Quomodo habueris, fili, sic fac eleemosynam. ⁹ Si tibi largior
fuerit substantia, plus ex illa fac eleemosynam : si exiguum
habueris, ex hoc ipso exiguo communica ; et ne timueris, fili,
cum facies eleemosynam. ¹⁰ Praemium bonum repones tibi in
die necessitatis : ¹¹ quoniam eleemosyna a morte liberat, et
non patitur ire in tenebras. ¹² Munus bonum est eleemosyna
omnibus qui faciunt illam, coram summo Deo. ¹³ Adtende tibi,
fili, ab omni fornicatione : uxorem proximam accipe ex semine
parentum tuorum, et noli sumere uxorem alienam, quae non est
ex tribu parentum tuorum : quoniam filii prophetarum sumus,
qui in veritate prophetaverunt priores. Noe prophetavit prior,
et Abraham, et Isaac, et Jacob, parentes nostri a principio
saeculi. Rememorare, fili, quoniam hi omnes acceperunt uxores
ex genere patrum suorum, et benedicti sunt in filiis suis, et
semen filiorum possidebit haereditatem terrae. ¹⁴ Et tu, fili,
dilige fratres tuos ; et noli superbo corde agere cum filiabus
filiorum populi tui, ut non accipias unam ex illis : quoniam
superbia, perditio et inconstantia magna est ; et luxuria, dimi-
nutio et impietas magna est. ¹⁵ Mercedem omni homini, qui-
cunque penes te operatus fuerit, redde eadem die, et non maneat
penes te merces hominis : et non minorabitur merces tua, si
servieris Deo in veritate. ¹⁶ Adtende tibi, fili, in omnibus operibus tuis, et esto sapiens in omnibus sermonibus tuis : et
quod oderis, alio ne feceris. Noli bibere vinum in ebrietate,
et non comitetur tecum ulla nequitia in omni vita tua. ¹⁷ De
pane tuo communica esurientibus, et vestimentis tuis nudos tege.
Ex omnibus quaecunque tibi abundaverint, fili, fac eleemosynam;
et non videat oculus tuus, cum facis eleemosynam. ¹⁸ Funde
vinum tuum et panem tuum super sepulcra justorum, et noli
illud dare peccatoribus. ¹⁹ Consilium ab homine sapiente inquire, et noli contemnere ; quoniam omne consilium utile est.
²⁰ Omni tempore benedic Deo : et postula ab illo, ut dirigantur
viae tuae, et omnes semitae tuae et cogitationes bene dispo-

nantur: quoniam caeterae nationes non habent bonam cogita-
tionem. Quem ergo voluerit, ipse allevat; et quem voluerit,
ipse demergit usque ad inferos deorsum: et nunc, fili mi, memor
esto praeceptorum meorum, et non deleantur de corde tuo.
²¹ Nunc igitur, fili, indico tibi commendasse me decem talenta
argenti Gabelo filio Gabahel, in Rages civitate Medorum.
²³ Noli ergo vereri, fili, quia pauperem vitam gessimus: habebis
multa bona, si timueris Deum, et recesseris ab omni peccato, et
bene egeris.

Caput V.

¹ Tunc Thobias respondit Thobi patri suo, dicens: Omnia
quaecunque praecepisti mihi, pater, sic faciam. ² Quomodo
autem potero hanc pecuniam recipere ab illo? neque enim me
ille novit, neque ego illum: vel quod signum dabo illi, ut me
cognoscat, et credat, et det mihi hanc pecuniam? Sed neque
vias regionis illius novi. ³ Et respondit Thobi filio suo, dicens:
Chirographum suum dedit mihi, et meum similiter accepit, et
divisit in duas partes: unum accepi ego, et alium posui cum
ipsa pecunia; et jam anni sunt viginti, ex quo penes illum de-
posui hanc pecuniam. ⁴ Nunc itaque, fili, inquire aliquem
hominem fidelem, qui eat tecum accepta mercede: et dum
adhuc vivo, recipe pecuniam ab illo. ⁵ Et exiit Thobias quaerere
hominem, qui eum duceret in regionem Mediam, et qui maxime
haberet notitiam viae regionis illius: et invenit Raphahel angelum stantem. ⁶ Et ignorans illum angelum Dei esse, dixit illi:
Unde es, juvenis? ⁷ Et ille respondit, dicens: Ex filiis Israel
fratrum tuorum veni huc, ut operer. Et dixit illi Thobias:
Nosti viam quae ducit in regionem Mediam? ⁸ Et ille dixit:
Multa ego novi: et teneo vias omnes, et aliquoties ivi in illam
regionem; et mansi apud Gabelum fratrem nostrum, qui com-
moratur in Rages civitate Medorum: et est iter bidui ex
Bathanis, usque Rages civitatem Phagar, quae posita est in
monte; et est Bathanu in medio campo. ⁹ Et dixit illi Thobias:
Sustine, juvenis, donec intrem, et hoc ipsum patri meo nunciem:

necessarium est enim ut eas mecum, et dabo tibi mercedem
tuam. Et respondens Raphahel angelus, dixit: Ecce sustineo
te, noli tardare. ¹⁰ Et introivit Thobias, et renuntiavit Tobi
patri suo, dicens: Ecce inveni hominem ex fratribus nostris, qui
eat mecum. Et ille dixit: Roga mihi hominem, fili, ut sciam
ex qua tribu sit; et an fidelis sit, cui tu committaris. Et exiit
Thobias, et vocavit illum, dicens: Juvenis intra, pater meus te
rogat. ¹¹ Et cum intrasset, prior Thobis salutavit eum. Et ille
dixit: Gaudium tibi semper sit, frater. ¹² Et respondit Thobis,
et dixit: Ut quid mihi gaudium? homo sum invalidus oculis,
et non video lumen coelorum, sed in tenebris positus sum,
sicut mortuus inter vivos: vocem hominum audio, et ipsos non
video. ¹³ Et dixit illi Raphahel angelus: Forti animo esto, in
proximo est ut a Deo cureris. ¹⁴ Et respondit illi Thobis:
Thobias filius meus vult ire in regionem Mediam; si poteris ire
cum illo, et deducere illum, dabo tibi mercedem tuam, frater.
¹⁵ Et dixit Raphahel angelus: Potero ire cum illo: quoniam
novi omnes vias, et aliquoties ivi in regionem Mediam; et
perambulavi omnes campos ejus, et montes, et omnes comme-
atus ejus bene teneo. ¹⁶ Et dixit Thobis: Frater, ex quo
genere es, et ex qua tribu? narra mihi. ¹⁷ Et ille dixit: Quid
necesse est te scire genus meum, vel tribum meam? merce-
narium desideras; genus et tribum meam cur quaeris? ¹⁸ Sed
si valde exigis, ego sum Azarias Annaniae magni filius, ex
fratribus tuis. ¹⁹ Et dixit illi Thobis: Salvus et sanus venias,
frater. Sed peto ne irascaris quod voluerim vere scire de genere
tuo. Tu ergo ex fratribus meis es, de genere bono et optimo:
Nosti Annaniam et Nathan, duos filios Semeiae magni viri, qui
et ipsi mecum ibant in Hierusalem, et adorabant ibi mecum,
et non exerraverunt? Hi omnes fratres nostri, optimi sunt.
Ex bona radice es, frater, salvus eas, et salvus venias. Et
adjecit, dicens: Ego tibi dabo, mercedis nomine, didragmam
diurnam, et quaecunque necessaria sunt tibi, et filio meo similiter: et vade cum illo, et adjiciam tibi ad mercedem tuam.
²⁰ Et dixit illi Raphahel angelus: Ibo cum illo, ne timueris:

salvi ibimus, et salvi revertemur ad te cum pace, quoniam via tuta est. ˙ ²¹ Et Thobis dixit : Bene iter age, frater et contingat tibi. Et vocavit Thobiam filium suum, et dixit illi : Praepara te, et exi cum fratre tuo : Deus autem qui in coelo est perducat vos ibi cum pace, et reducat salvos, et angelus illius comitetur vobiscum cum sanitate. ²² Et praeparavit se ad viam Thobias, et exiit ut iret : et osculatus est patrem suum et matrem ; et dixit illi Thobis pater suus : Vade, fili, salvus et sanus venias. ²³ Et lacrymata est mater illius, et dixit patri ejus : Quo misisti filium nostrum ? Nonne ipsa est virga manus nostrae, et ipse intrat et exit coram nobis ? ²⁴ Nunquam esset pecunia illa, sed purgamento sit. ²⁵ Quo modo datum est a Domino vivere, hoc sufficiebat nobis. ²⁶ Et dixit illi Thobis : Noli vereri, salvus ibit filius noster, et salvus revertetur ad nos, et oculi tui videbunt illum illa die qua venerit. ²⁷ Nihil timueris de illo, soror ; angelus bonus comitetur cum illo, et bene disponet viam illius, et revertetur sanus. ²⁸ Et cessavit plorare.

Caput VI.

¹ Et profectus est filius illorum, et angelus cum illo, et canis secutus est eos : et ibant pariter, et comprehendit illos proxima nox, et manserunt super flumen Tigrim. ² Et descendit Thobias lavare pedes suos in flumine, et exsilivit piscis de aqua magnus, et circumplexus est pedes ejus : pene puerum devoraverat. ³ Et exclamavit puer. ⁴ Et dixit illi angelus : Comprehende et tene illum. Et comprehendit puer piscem, et eduxit illum in terram. ⁵ Et dixit angelus puero : Exintera hunc piscem, et tolle fel, et cor, et jecor illius, et repone et habe tecum : sunt enim necessaria haec ad medicamenta utilia : et caetera interanea projice. ⁶ Et exinteravit puer piscem illum, et tulit fel, et cor, et jecor : et partem piscis assaverunt, et tulerunt in via ; caetera autem salierunt : et coeperunt iter agere, donec pervenirent in regionem Medorum. ⁷ Et interrogavit puer angelum, dicens : Azarias frater, quod remedium est hoc fel, cor, et jecor piscis ? ⁸ Et angelus dixit : Cor et jecor fumigatur coram viro, et muliere,

qui incursum daemonis aut spiritum immundum habet; et
fugiet ab illo omnis incursus, et non apparebit in aeternum.
⁹. Et fel facit ad unguendos oculos homini, cui fuerint albugines,
vel ad flandum in ipsis oculorum maculis, ut ad sanitatem per-
veniant.   ¹⁰ Et postquam intraverunt in regionem Mediam,
adpropinquaverunt civitati Bathanis.   ¹¹ Et dixit Raphahel
angelus: Raguhel, penes quem hac nocte manere nos oportet,
homo est propinquus tuus, et habet filiam speciosam nomine
Sarram, sed neque masculum ullum, neque feminam aliam
praeter illam habet.   ¹² Et tu proximus es illius super omnes
homines, ut possideas eam, et haereditatem illius, et omnem
substantiam patris ejus: accipe illam uxorem.   Etenim puella
haec sapiens, fortis et bona valde, et constabilita; et pater ipsius
diligit illam, et quaecunque possedit illi tradet.   Tibi ergo
destinata est haereditas patris ejus, et te oportet accipere illam.
¹³ Et nunc audi me, frater, et loquere de illa hac nocte, et acci-
piemus tibi illam uxorem: et cum regressi fuerimus ex Rages,
faciemus nuptias ejus.   Scio autem quia Raguhel non negabit
illam tibi: novit enim quia si dederit illam viro alio, morte
periet secundum judicium libri Moysi: et quia scit tibi maxime
aptam esse haereditatem illius, magis quam alicui homini.   Nunc
ergo, frater, audi me, et loquamur de hac puella, et desponse-
mus illam tibi: et reversi ex Rages, ducemus eam nobiscum
in domum tuam.   ¹⁴ Tunc respondit Thobias Raphahel angelo,
et dixit: Azarias frater, audivi quoniam jam tradita est viris
septem, et mortui sunt in cubiculo nocte, ea hora qua cum illa
fuerunt: audivi etiam quosdam dicentes, quoniam daemonium
est quod illos occidit.   ¹⁵ Et nunc timeo hoc daemonium, quoniam diligit illam: et ipsam quidem non vexat, sed eum qui
illi adplicitus fuerit, ipsum occidit.   Unicus sum patri meo;
ne forte moriar, et deducam patris mei vitam, et matris meae
cum dolore ad inferos: sed neque habent alium filium, qui
sepeliat illos, et possideat haereditatem illorum.   ¹⁶ Et dixit
Raphahel angelus: Memor esto mandatorum patris tui, quoniam
praecepit tibi accipere te debere uxorem de domo patris tui.

Et nunc audi me, frater, noli computare daemonium illud : sed postula illam, et scio quoniam dabitur tibi hac nocte uxor. [18][19] Et cum intraveris in cubiculum, tolle jecor et cor piscis illius, et pone super carbones : et odor manabit, et odorabitur illud daemonium, et fugiet, et non apparebit circa illam omnino in perpetuum. [19][18] Et cum coeperis velle esse cum illa, surgite primo ambo, et deprecamini Dominum coeli, ut detur vobis misericordia et sanitas. [20] Noli timere, tibi enim destinata est ante saecula : et tu illam sanabis, et ibit tecum ; [21] et credo quoniam habebis ex illa filios, et erunt tibi sicut fratres. [22] Et cum audisset Thobias sermones Raphahel angeli, quoniam soror est illius, et de domo seminis patris illius, haesit cordi ejus.

Caput VII.

[1] Et cum venissent in civitatem Ecbatanan, dicit Thobias angelo : Azarias frater, duc me viam rectam ad Raguhelem. Et venerunt, et invenerunt illum sedentem in atrio, circa ostium domus suae, et salutaverunt illum priores. Et dixit Raguhel : Bene valeatis, fratres, intrate salvi et sani : et induxit illos in domum suam. [2] Et dixit Annae uxori suae : Quam similis est hic juvenis Thobis consobrini mei ! [3] Et interrogavit illos Anna, dicens : Unde estis, fratres ? Et illi dixerunt : Ex filiis Nepthalim nos sumus, ex captivis Ninive. [4] Tunc illa dixit : Nostis Thobin fratrem nostrum ? Et dixerunt : Novimus. Et illa dixit : Fortis est ? Et illi dixerunt : Fortis est et vivat. [5] Tunc Thobias dixit : Pater meus est, de quo quaeris. [6] Et exsiliit Raguhel, et osculatus est illum lacrymans, [7] et dixit : Benedictio tibi sit, fili, quoniam boni et optimi viri filius es tu. O infelicitas malorum, quia excaecatus est vir justus et faciens eleemosynas ! Et incubuit lacrymans super collum Thobiae filii fratris sui. [8] Et Anna uxor ejus et Sarra filia eorum lacrymatae sunt. [9] Et occiderunt arietem, et susceperunt illos libenter : et postquam laverunt, discubuerunt ad coenandum. [10] Et dixit Thobias ad Raphahel angelum : Azarias frater, dic Raguheli ut det mihi Sarram sororem meam. Et audivit Raguhel hunc sermonem,

et dixit illi: Manduca et bibe, et suaviter tibi sit hac nocte: non est enim alius cui oporteat accipere Sarram filiam meam quam tu; similiter et mihi non licet illam dare alio viro quam tibi: tu proximus mihi es, et tibi Sarra. [11] Verum autem tibi dicam, fili: tradidi illam jam viris septem, fratribus nostris; et omnes mortui sunt dum cum illa secedunt. Nunc ergo, fili, manduca et bibe. Et dixit Thobias: Hic ego non edam quicquam neque bibam donec mecum rem confirmes. [13] Et Raguhel dixit: Ne dubites, fili, facio quod vis. Et his dictis adjecit, dicens: [14] Tibi Sarra destinata est secundum judicium libri Moysi, et de coelo judicatum est tibi illam dari. Accipe sororem tuam, amodo tu illius frater es, et haec tua soror est: datur tibi ex hodierno et in aeternum. Et Dominus coeli bene disponat vobis hanc noctem, et faciat vobis misericordiam et pacem. [15] Et accersivit Raguhel Sarram filiam suam, et accessit ad illum: et, adprehensa manu virginis, tradidit eam illi, et dixit: Ecce, accipe secundum legem et judicium quod scriptum est in lege Moysi, dare tibi hanc uxorem. Habe itaque, et duc illam ad patrem tuum, fili, salvus et sanus: et Deus de coelo det vobis bonum iter, et pacem. [16] Et vocavit matrem et puellam, et praecepit afferri chartam, ut faceret conscriptionem conjugii, quemadmodum tradidit illam uxorem secundum judicium libri Moysi. Et attulit mater illius chartam, et ille scripsit, et signavit. [17] Et ex illa hora coeperunt manducare et bibere. [18] Et vocavit Raguhel Annam uxorem suam, et dixit illi: Praepara cubiculum aliud, et introduc illuc puellam. Et abiit in cubiculum, et stravit, sicut illi dictum est. [19] Et introduxit filiam suam, et lacrymata est causa illius: et extersit lacrymas, [20] et dixit illi: Forti animo esto, filia: Dominus coeli det tibi gaudium pro taedio tuo. Et exiit inde.

Caput VIII.

[1] Et postquam consummaverunt coenam, voluerunt dormire; et deduxerunt juvenem, et induxerunt illum in cubiculum. [2] Et rememoratus est Thobias sermonum Raphahel angeli: et

sustulit de sacculo quem habebat cor et jecor piscis, et imposuit super carbones vivos. [3] Et odor piscis prohibuit daemonium, et refugit in superiores partes Aegypti. Et abiit Raphahel angelus, et conligavit eum ibi, et reversus est continuo. [4] Et exierunt, et clauserunt ostium cubiculi. Et surrexit Thobias de lecto, et dixit Sarrae : Surge, soror, oremus et deprecemur Deum, ut faciat misericordiam nobiscum. [6] Et surrexerunt, et coeperunt orare et deprecari Dominum, ut daretur illis sanitas. [7] Et dixerunt: Benedictus es, Domine Deus patrum nostrorum, et benedictum nomen tuum in omnia saecula saeculorum : et benedicant tibi coeli, et omnis creatura tua. [8] Tu fecisti Adam, et dedisti illi adjutorium Evam, et ex his multiplicasti semen hominum. [9] Et nunc, Domine, tu scis, quoniam non luxuriae causa accipio uxorem sororem meam, sed ipsa veritate, [10] ut miserearis nostri, Domine, et consenescamus pariter sani cum pace ; et da nobis filios in benedictione. Et dixerunt, Amen : et receperunt se. [11] Et surrexit Raguhel, et accersivit servos suos, et abierunt cum illo, et foderunt foveam per noctem. [12] Dicebat enim : Ne forte moriatur Thobias, et omnibus fiam derisio et opprobrium. [13] Et consummaverunt fossuram. Reversus est Raguhel domum, et vocavit uxorem suam, et dixit : [14] Mitte unam ex ancillis ad cubiculum, et videat si vivit, an mortuus est, ut sepeliamus illum nemine sciente. [15] Et misit unam ex ancillis. Et accensa lucerna, aperuit ostium, et intravit, et invenit illos pariter dormientes. [16] Et reversa, nunciavit illum vivere, et nihil mali passum : et benedixit Raguhel Deum coeli, [17] dicens : Benedictus es, Domine, omni benedictione sancta et munda : et benedicant tibi omnes electi tui, et omnis creatura tua benedicat tibi, in omnia saecula saeculorum. Benedictus es, quoniam laetificasti me, et non contigit mihi sicut putabam; [18] sed secundum magnam misericordiam tuam egisti nobiscum. [19] Benedictus es, quia misertus es duorum unicorum. Fac cum illis, Domine, misericordiam, et da sanitatem : et consumma vitam eorum cum misericordia et laetitia. [20] Et praecepit servis suis, ut replerent fossam quam fecerant, priusquam lucesceret. ²¹ Et praecepit uxori suae ut faceret panes multos. ²² Et abiit ipse ad gregem, et adduxit vaccas duas et quatuor arietes, et jussit praeparari. ²³ Et vocavit Thobiam, et juravit illi, dicens : His diebus quatuordecim hinc non recedes ; sed hic eris manducans et bibens mecum, et laetificabis animam filiae meae, multis adflictam doloribus. ²⁴ Et ex eo quod possideo accipe partem dimidiam, et vade salvus et sanus cum pace ad patrem tuum ; et alia dimidia pars, cum mortui fuerimus ego et uxor mea, vestra erit. Forti animo esto, fili, ego pater tuus sum, et Anna mater tua ; tui sumus nos, et sororis tuae, amodo et in perpetuo.

Caput IX.

¹ Tunc accersivit Thobias Raphahel angelum, et dixit illi : ³ Azarias frater, adsume tecum hinc servos quatuor, et camelos duos, et perveni in civitatem Rages ad Gabelum : et da illi chirographum suum, et recipe pecuniam, et accersi illum ad nuptias. ⁴ Scis enim quoniam numerat dies pater meus : et si tardavero una plus die, contristabo animam ejus. ⁵ Sed vides quomodo Raguhel juraverit, cujus jusjurandum spernere non possumus. ⁶ Et abiit Raphahel angelus, cum quatuor servis et duobus camelis, in civitatem Rages : et manserunt penes Gabelum, et dedit illi Raphahel chirographum suum. ⁷ Et indicavit illi de Thobia filio Thobi, quoniam accepit uxorem filiam Raguhel, et rogat illum ad nuptias. Et continuo surrexit, et adsignavit illi saccos cum suis sigillis, et composuerunt illos supra camelos ; et vigilaverunt simul, et venerunt ad nuptias. ⁸ Et invenit Gabelus Thobiam discumbentem : et exsilivit, et salutavit, et osculatus est eum : et lacrymatus est Gabelus, et benedixit Deum, ⁹ dicens : Benedictus Dominus qui dedit tibi pacem, bone et optime vir, quoniam boni et optimi et justi viri, eleemosynas facientis, filius es : et benedictus tu, fili. ¹⁰ Det tibi benedictionem Dominus coeli, et uxori tuae, et patri et matri uxoris tuae : et benedictus Deus, quoniam video Thobi consubrini mei similem.

Caput X.

[1] Et quotidie computabat Thobis dies, quibus iret et reverteretur filius ejus. Et postquam consummati sunt dies, et filius ejus non veniebat, dixit: Nunquid detentus est Thobias? [2] Aut forte Gabelus mortuus est, et nemo illi reddidit pecuniam. [3] Et contristari coepit; et Anna uxor illius dicebat: Periit filius meus, et jam non est inter vivos: quare tardat? [4] Et coepit plorare, et lugere filium suum, dicens: Vae mihi, fili, quae te dimisi ire, lumen oculorum meorum! [6] Cui Thobis dicebat: Tace, noli contristari, soror, salvus est filius noster; sed aliqua forsitan mora detinet illos: homo enim qui cum illo ivit fidelis est, et ex fratribus nostris. Noli taediari pro illo, soror; jam venit. [7] Et illa dicebat: Tace, molestus es mihi: noli me seducere, periit filius meus. Et exsiliens circumspiciebat viam qua filius ejus profectus erat, et nihil gustabat: et cum occidisset sol, introibat, et lugebat lacrymans tota nocte, et non dormiebat. [8] [9] Et ut consummati sunt quatuordecim dies nuptiarum de quibus juraverat Raguhel, exiit ad illum Thobias, et dixit illi: Dimitte me; scio enim quia pater meus et mater mea non credunt se visuros me. Nunc itaque peto, pater, et dimittas me, ut eam ad patrem meum: jam tibi indicavi quomodo illum reliquerim. [9] [8] Et dixit Raguhel Thobiae: Remane hic penes me, et ego nuncios mittam patri tuo, et indicabunt illi de te. Et ille dixit: In totum, pater, peto, ut dimittas me hinc ad patrem meum. [10] Et continuo surgens Raguhel tradidit Thobiae Sarram filiam suam, et dimidiam partem substantiae suae, pueros et puellas, oves et boves, asinos et camelos, vestes, vasa, et pecuniam: et dimisit illum salvum sanum, et vale illi fecit, [11] et dixit: Vade, fili, salvus sanus, Dominus coeli bene disponat iter tuum, et Sarrae uxori tuae, et videam ex vobis filios antequam moriar. [12] Et adprehendit illam, et salutans osculatus est Sarram filiam suam, [13] et dixit illi: Filia, honorem habe socero tuo et socrui tuae: ipsi amodo sunt parentes tui, tanquam pater tuus et mater tua, qui te

genuerunt. Vade salva, filia, audiam de te auditionem bonam
in vita mea et gaudium : et osculatus est eam, et dimisit illam.
Et Anna dixit Thobiae: Fili et frater dilecte, salvum te perducat Dominus coeli, et det mihi ut videam filios de Sarra filia
mea antequam moriar, ut delecter coram Domino coeli. Ego
trado tibi Sarram filiam meam, tanquam bonum depositum ; et
non·vexes eam omnibus diebus vitae tuae. Vade, fili, salvus et
sanus : ego mater tua amodo, et Sarra uxor tua. Diligat te
Dominus et illam, ut sitis in loco sanctitatis omnibus diebus
vitae vestrae. Et osculata est utrosque, et dimisit illos sanos.
Et discessit Thobias a Raguhele, gaudens et benedicens Deum
coeli et terrae, regem omnium, quia direxit viam ejus : et benedixit Raguheli et Annae uxori illius, et dixit : Injunctum est
mihi a Domino honorari vos omnibus diebus vitae vestrae.

Caput XI.

¹ Et profecti sunt, et ibant donec venirent Charam, quae
civitas est contra Niniven. ² Tunc dixit Raphahel: Thobias
frater, nescis quomodo reliqueris patrem tuum ? ³ Praecedamus
uxorem tuam, et eamus, et praeparemus domum, dum prose-
quitur nos puella. ⁴ Et praecesserunt pariter, et dixit illi
angelus: Tolle tecum de felle illo, et habe. Et abiit cum
illis et canis. ⁵ Et Anna sedebat in via, circumspiciens adven-
tum filii sui. ⁶ Et cognovit illum venientem, et dixit patri
ejus : Ecce filius tuus venit, et homo qui cum illo erat. ⁷ Et
Raphahel dixit Thobiae: Antequam adpropinquemus patri tuo,
scio enim quia oculi ejus aperientur ; ⁸ adsperge ergo oculis ejus
fel piscis, et insidet medicamentum ; et decoriabis albugines ab
oculis ejus, et respiciet pater tuus, et videbit lumen. ⁹ Et
adcurrit ei mater sua, et irruit collo filii sui, et dixit illi: Fili,
video te, amodo libenter moriar ; et lacrymata est: Thobias
etiam lacrymatus est. ¹⁰ Et surrexit Thobis, et offendebat pedi-
bus : et egressus est atrium, et occurrit illi Thobias, ferens
fel piscis in manibus suis. ¹³ Et insufflavit in oculis Thobis
patris sui, et adprehendit eum, et dixit illi: Forti animo esto,

pater : et injecit medicamentum in oculis ejus, et morsum illi praebebat. [14] Et decoriavit duabus manibus albugines oculorum illius, [15] et vidit filium suum, et irruit collo ejus, et lacrymatus est. [16] Et benedixit Deum, [17] et dixit : Video te, fili : Benedictus Deus, et benedictum nomen illius magnum, et benedicti omnes sancti angeli ejus. Sit nomen illius sanctum in omnia saecula saeculorum, quoniam ipse flagellavit me, et ipse misertus est mei : ecce ego video Thobiam filium meum. [18] Et introivit Thobias et Anna uxor ejus in domum, gaudentes, et benedicentes Deum toto ore suo, pro omnibus quae sibi evenerant. [19] Et indicavit patri suo Thobias, quoniam perfecta est via illius bene a Domino Deo, et quia adtulit pecuniam ; et quemadmodum accepit Sarram filiam Raguhelis uxorem, et quia venit et ipsa, et jam proximo est portae Ninive. Et gavisi sunt Thobis et Anna, et exierunt in obviam nurui suae : et videbant Thobin, qui erant in porta Ninive, venientem, et ambulantem cum omni virtute sua, nemine dante ei manum ; et mirabantur. Et confitebatur Thobis, et benedicebat magna voce Deum, et ambulabat cum gaudio coram omnibus, quoniam misertus est illius Deus, et aperuit oculos ejus. Et ut adpropinquavit Thobias, adducens Sarram uxorem suam, benedixit illi Thobis, dicens : Intra sana, Sarra filia. Benedictus Deus, qui adduxit te ad nos, et benedictus pater tuus, et mater tua : et benedictus Thobias filius meus, et benedicta tu filia ; intra in domum tuam sana, in benedictione et gaudio. In illa die erat gaudium magnum omnibus Judaeis qui erant in Ninive. [20] Et venit Achicarus, et Nabal avunculus illius, gaudentes ad Thobin. [21] Et consummatae sunt nuptiae cum gaudio septem diebus, et data sunt illi munera multa.

Caput XII.

[1] Et postquam consummatae sunt nuptiae, vocavit Thobis Thobiam filium suum, et dixit illi : Homini illi qui tecum fuit, reddamus honorem suum, et adjiciamus illi ad mercedem. [2] Et ille dixit : Pater, quantum illi dabo ? non enim satis est si

dedero illi ex his quae mecum adtuli dimidiam partem. ³ Duxit enim me sanum et reduxit, et uxorem meam curavit, et pecuniam mecum adtulit, et te curavit. Quantum illi dabo mercedem? ⁴ Et dixit Thobis: Justum est illum, fili, dimidium horum quae tecum attulit accipere. ⁵ Et vocavit illum Thobias, et dixit ei: Accipe dimidium horum quae tecum adtulisti: haec erit merces tua, et vade sanus. ⁶ Tunc Raphahel vocavit ambos abscondite, et dixit illis: Deum benedicite, et illi confitemini, et ipsius majestati date honorem; et confitemini illi coram omnibus viventibus, quia fecit vobiscum bona, ut benedicatis Deo, et decantetis nomini ejus; et sermones de operibus ejus honorifice ostendite, et confitemini illi. ⁷ Quoniam sacramentum regis bonum est abscondere: opera autem Dei revelare et confiteri honorificum est. ⁸ Bona est oratio cum jejunio, et eleemosyna cum justitia: super utrumque autem melius est modicum cum justitia quam plurimum cum iniquitate. Bonum est facere eleemosynam magis quam thesauros auri condere: ⁹ quia eleemosyna a morte liberat, et ipsa purgat peccata. Qui faciunt eleemosynam et miserationem et justitiam, saturabuntur vita aeterna. ¹⁰ Qui faciunt peccatum et iniquitatem, hostes sunt animae suae. ¹¹ Omnem veritatem vobis manifestabo, et non abscondam a vobis ullum sermonem. Et jam vobis demonstravi et dixi, quia sacramentum regis bonum abscondere, opera autem Dei revelare et confiteri honorificum est. ¹² Et tunc quando orabas tu, et Sarra, ego obtuli memoriam orationis vestrae in conspectu claritatis Dei, et legi: et cum sepelires mortuos, similiter; et quia non es cunctatus exsurgere, et relinquere prandium tuum, et abiisti, et sepelisti mortuum. ¹⁴ Et missus sum tentare te, et Sarram nurum tuam. ¹⁵ Ego enim sum Raphahel, unus de septem angelis sanctis, qui adsistimus et conversamur ante claritatem Dei. ¹⁶ Et conturbati sunt utrique, et ceciderunt in faciem, et timuerunt. ¹⁷ Et dixit illis Raphahel: Nolite timere, pax vobiscum, Deum benedicite in omni aevo. ¹⁸ Etenim cum essem vobiscum, non mea gratia eram sed voluntate Dei: ipsi ergo benedicite, et omnibus

diebus decantate ei.   [19] Et videbatis me quia manducabam; sed
visu vestro videbatis.   [20] Et nunc surgite a terra, et confitemini
Deo. Ecce ego ascendo ad eum, qui me misit: scribite ergo
omnia quae contigerunt vobis.   [21] Et ascendit: et surrexerunt,
et non potuerunt illum videre.   [22] Et benedicebant et decanta-
bant Deo, et confitebantur illi in omnibus operibus magnis
illius, quia apparuit illis angelus Dei.

Caput XIII.

[1] Tunc locutus est Thobis, et scripsit orationem in laetitia,
et dixit: Benedictus es, Deus, quia magnus es, et vivis in aeternum.   Quoniam in omnia saecula regnum est illius: [2] quia ipse
flagellat et miseretur: deducet usque ad inferos deorsum, et
reducet a perditione, majestate sua: et non est qui effugiat
manum ejus.   [3] Confitemini illi, filii Israel, coram nationibus,
[4] quia ipse dispersit vos in illis; et ibi adnuntiate misericordiam
ejus, et exaltate illum coram omni vivente: quoniam ipse est
Dominus Deus noster, et ipse pater noster, et Deus in omnia
saecula saeculorum.   [5] Flagellavit vos ob iniquitates vestras: et
omnium miserebitur vestrum, et colliget vos ab omnibus nationibus ubicunque dispersi fueritis.   Cum conversi fueritis ad
illum ex toto corde vestro, ut faciatis coram illo veritatem;
tunc revertetur ad vos, et non avertet faciem suam a vobis
amplius.   [6] Et nunc aspicite quae fecit Dominus vobis, et confitemini illi ex toto corde vestro, ut faciatis coram illo veritatem:
et benedicite Domino in justitia, et exaltate regem saeculorum.
[7] Ego in terra captivitatis meae confiteor illi, et ostendo vir-
tutem ipsius, et majestatem ejus coram natione peccatrice.
[8] Convertimini, peccatores, et facite justitiam coram illo: qui
scit si velit ut faciat vobiscum misericordiam? [9] Ego et anima
mea regi coeli laetationem dicimus, et anima mea laetabitur
omnibus diebus vitae meae.   [10] Benedicite Domino omnes electi,
et omnes laudate majestatem ejus: agite dies laetitiae, et confitemini illi.   [11] Hierusalem, civitas sancta, flagellavit te in
operibus manuum tuarum.   [12] Confitere Domino in bono, et

benedic Domino saeculorum, ut iterum tabernaculum tuum aedificetur in te cum gaudio, et laetos faciat in te omnes captivos, et diligat omnes miseros in omnia saecula saeculorum. [13] Luce splendida fulgebunt, in omnibus finibus terrae. [14] Nationes multae venient tibi ex longinquo, habitare a novissimis partibus terrae ad nomen Dei mei; et munera sua in manibus habentes, regi coeli et terrae in laetitia offerentes. [15] Et nomen magnum erit in saecula saeculorum. [16] Maledicti omnes qui spernunt te, et omnes qui blasphemant te: maledicti erunt omnes qui odiunt te, et omnes qui dixerint verbum durum, et omnes qui deponunt te et destruunt muros tuos, et omnes qui subvertunt turres tuas, et omnes qui incendunt habitationes tuas: et benedicti erunt omnes qui aedificant te, in aevum. [17] Tunc gaude et laetare in filiis justorum, quoniam omnes colligentur, et benedicent Domino aeterno. [18] Felices qui diligunt te, et qui gaudent in pace tua. Beati omnes homines qui contristabuntur in omnibus flagellis tuis, quoniam in te gaudebunt, et videbunt omne gaudium tuum in aeternum. [19] Anima mea, benedic Domino regi magno, quia liberavit Hierusalem, et aedificabit iterum domus illius in omnia saecula saeculorum. [20] Felix ero si fuerint reliquiae de semine meo ad videndam claritatem tuam, et confitendum nomini regis coeli. [21] Ostia Hierusalem sapphiro et zmaragdo aedificabuntur: ex lapide pretioso omnes muri tui, et turres Hierusalem auro aedificabuntur, et propugnacula ejus auro mundo. [22] Et plateae Hierusalem carbunculo lapide sternentur: et ostia illius canticum laetitiae dicent, et omnes vici ejus loquentur. [23] Benedictus Dominus, qui exaltat te, et benedictus in omnia saecula saeculorum: quoniam in te benedicet nomen sanctum suum in aeternum.

Caput IV.

[1] Et ut consummati sunt sermones confessionis Thobi, [2] mortuus est in pace, annorum centum duodecim, et sepultus est praeclare in Ninive. [3] Quinquaginta autem et octo annorum erat, cum oculis captus est; et quinquaginta quatuor annis,

postquam lucem recepit, vixit, in omnibus faciens eleemosynas.
⁴ Et proposuit magis Deum colere, et confiteri magnitudinem
ejus. ⁵ Et cum moriretur Thobis, accersiit Thobiam filium suum,
et septem filios ejus, et praecepit illis, dicens : ⁶ Fili, dilige filios
tuos, et recurre in regionem Medorum : quoniam credo ego
verbo Dei, quod locutus est in Niniven ; quia omnia erunt, et
veniet adhuc super Assur et Niniven, quae locuti sunt prophetae
Israel, quos misit Dominus. Omnia evenient, nihilque minuetur
ex omnibus verbis : sed omnia contingent temporibus suis, et
in Media erit salus, magis quam in Assyriis, et quam in Baby-
lone : quia scio ego et credo quoniam omnia quae dixit Dominus,
erunt, et perficientur ; et non excedet verbum de sermonibus
Dei. Et fratres nostri, qui habitant in terra Israel, omnes
dispergentur, et ex illis captivi ducentur ad terram optimam.
⁷ Et erit omnis terra Israel deserta, et domus Dei, quae in illa
est, incendetur ; et erit deserta usque in tempus. Et iterum
miserebitur illorum Deus in terra Israel, et iterum aedificabunt
domum, sed non ut prius ; quoadusque repleatur tempus male-
dictionum. Et postea revertentur a captivitate sua, et omnes
aedificabunt Hierusalem honorifice, et domus Dei aedificabitur
in ea, et in omnia saecula saeculorum aedificabitur, sicut locuti
sunt de illa omnes prophetae Israel. Et tunc omnes nationes
terrae convertentur ad timendum Deum vere, ⁸ et relinquent
omnia idola sua, quae seducunt illos falso errore : et omnes
benedicent Dominum in aeternum, et in justitia. Et omnes
filii Israel, qui liberabuntur in diebus illis, memores erunt Dei
in veritate : et colligentur, et venient in Hierusalem, et habita-
bunt in aeternum. In die illa, cum diligentia et omnis justitia
in illis erit, ⁹ et gaudebunt qui diligunt Deum verum : qui
autem faciunt iniquitatem et peccatum, deficient de terris
omnibus. ¹⁰ Et nunc, filii, vobis mando : Servite Domino in
veritate, et facite coram illo quod ipsi placet : ¹¹ et filiis vestris
mandate, ut faciant justitias et eleemosynas, et sint memores, et
benedicant nomini ipsius in omni tempore, in veritate, in toto
corde suo, et in tota virtute sua. ¹² Nunc vero, fili, exi a Ninive,

et noli manere hic : sed quacunque die sepelieris matrem tuam circa me, eodem die noli manere in finibus ejus : [13] video enim quia multa iniquitas est in illa, et fictio multa perficitur, et non confunduntur. Ecce filius Nabad, quid fecit Achicaro qui eum nutrivit, quem vivum deduxit in terram deorsum ? sed reddidit Deus malitiam illius ante faciem ipsius : et Achicar exiit ad lucem, Nabad autem intravit in tenebras aeternas, quia quaesivit Nabad Achicarum occidere. [14] Et abiit Thobias, postquam sepelivit parentes suos, et uxor ejus et filii in regionem Medorum, et habitavit in civitate Ecbathana, cum Raguhele socero suo : [15] et curam habebat senectutis eorum honorifice : et sepelivit illos Ecbathanis in regione Media : et haereditatem percepit domus Raguhel et Thobis patris sui. [16] Et mortuus est annorum centum decem et septem cum claritate. [17] Et antequam moriretur audivit perditionem Ninives ; et vidit captivitatem illius adductam in civitatem Medorum, quam adduxit Achicar rex Medorum : et benedixit Dominum in omnibus quae fecit in filiis Ninive et Assur, et gavisus est antequam moriretur in terra Ninive.

APPENDIX.

A. BEL AND THE DRAGON.

THE Midrash Rabbah de Rabbah on the verse ' And they cast him into the pit' (Gen. xxxvii. 24), in the section beginning 'And Jacob dwelt' (Gen. xxxvii. 1), says: 'I called upon thy name, O Lord, out of the low dungeon' (Lam. iii. 55). This is Daniel who prayed before the Holy One (blessed is he) out of the pit, and the Holy One (blessed is he) heard the voice of his prayer, and delivered him from the lions. This is what is written, ' Thou hast heard my voice,' etc., 'thou drewest near in the day that I called upon thee,' etc. (Lam. iii. 56, 57). And so he says, ' My God hath sent his angel, and hath shut the lions' mouths, that they have not hurt me, forasmuch as before him innocency was found in me' (Dan. vi. 23). And it was not sufficient that he delivered him, but he avenged him on his enemies. This is what is written, ' O Lord, thou hast pleaded the causes of my soul, thou hast redeemed my life' (Lam. iii. 58). And so he says, 'And the king commanded, and they brought those men which had accused Daniel, and they cast them into the den of lions, them, their children, and their wives; and the lions had the mastery of them, and brake all their bones in pieces or ever they came at the bottom of the den' (Dan. vi. 25). Behold, we find from Scripture that Daniel was delivered from the pit, and our Rabbis say that we have a tradition that Daniel was delivered a second time from the lions' pit in the days of Cyrus the Persian, because he would not believe in idol-worship. They say[1]. Therefore[2] it is said, ' They have cut off my life in the pit, and

---

[1] For the translation of the Syriac text, see the Preface, p. xiv, note 1.
[2] Page 43 of the text.

cast a stone upon me. Waters flowed over mine head; then I said, I am cut off. I called upon thy name, O Lord, out of the low pit' (Lam. iii. 53–55). We find that Daniel was twice cast into the pit, once in the days of Darius the Mede, and another time in the days of Cyrus the Persian, his father-in-law. Now on the first occasion he remained only one night in the pit, and was delivered; but on the second he remained in it seven days, and was delivered. This second history is not written in the sacred books. It would seem that, inasmuch as the righteous man is used to this miracle, it is sufficient to mention it once.

These[1] two histories, that is, the history of Bel, the image of the Chaldeans, and the story of the Dragon, are included by the Christians in the twenty-four books of the Prophets, together with three other books. The translator says that he has not found them in the sacred tongue.

B. EXTRACT FROM THE B'RESHITH RABBAH, § 68.

ANOTHER explanation. 'And behold the angels of God.' This is Daniel. 'Ascending and descending on it.' For he went up and brought forth from inside its mouth what it had swallowed. This is what the Scripture says: 'And I will punish Bel in Babylon, and I will bring forth out of his mouth that which he hath swallowed up' (Jer. li. 44). For Nebuchadnezzar had a dragon, which used to swallow up everything which they cast before it. Nebuchadnezzar said to Daniel, How great is its power, for it swallows up everything which they cast before it. Daniel said to him, Give me permission and I will weaken it. So he gave him permission. What did he do? He took straw, and hid nails in the midst thereof; then he cast it before it, and the nails pierced its intestines. This is what the Scripture says: 'And I will bring forth out of his mouth that which he hath swallowed up.'

---

[1] An addition by the copyist of the MS.

מעשה טוביה

או

ספר טוביה:

I. CHALDEE TEXT.

❖ מעשה טוביה ❖

והוא כתוב במדרש רבה דרבה פרשת ויצא יעקב פרשתא עֹ גבי
וכל אשר תתן לי עשר אעשרנו לך. עשר תעשר אמֹ להם משה עשר
ברכות תטלו אם תעשרו וכן יעקב אמֹ וכל אשר תתן לי עשר אעשרנו
לך עשר ברכות שתתן לי כמו שברכני אבי בזכות מה בזכות
5 אעשרנו לך :

א

עובדא הוה בחד חסידא ושמיה טובי בר טוביאל משבטא דנפתלי
דאשתבי ביומי שלמנאצר מלכא דאתור והוה יתיב בתשבי קרתא
דנפתלי דבגלילא וכל יומוי הליך טובי באורחא תקנא וכוון סגיאן עבד
לאחוהי ולעמיה דהוו עמיה בגלותא בנינוה בארעא דאתור. וכד הוה
10 טליא בארעא דישראל כל שבטא דנפתלי מרדו במלכותא דדוד ומנעו
גרמיהון למיסק לירושלם והוו דבחין לעגליא דעבד ירבעם מלכא דישראל
בבית אל ובדן והוא בלחודוהי אזל לירושלם בזמני מועדיא כמה
דכתוב בספר אוריתא דמשה והוה מוביל לתמן בכוריא ואפרשותא
ומעשריא ויהיב להון לכהניא וללויאי לכל חד וחד מאי דחזי ליה
15 ומעשרא תניינא ומעשרא עניא הוה אביל ויהיב בכל מה דכתו
בספרא דמשה והדין טובי אשתאר יתמא מאבוהי ורבת יתיה דבורה
אמיה דאבוהי והיא אדרכתיה. באורחא קשיטא וכד הוה גבר נסב
אתתא מזרעיתה ושמה חנה וילידת ליה בר וקרא שמיה טוביה : כד

A 2

אשתבי טובי יתב בנינוה קרתא רבתא וכל אחוהי וקריבוהי הוו מסאבין
נפשיהון ואכלין לחמא מן בני עממיא והוא לא אכל דהוה דחיל מן
אלהא ורחים יתיה בכל לביה: ועל דא יהב ליה אלהא חנא וחסדא
בעיני שלמנאצר מלכא דאתור ומני יתיה רבא על כל מה דהוה ליה
5 עד יום מותיה: ובההיא זימנא אפקיד בידא דגבאל אחוהי דקברי
קריביה בארעא דמדי בקורי רגש עשר ככרין דכספ: וביומי טובי מית
שלמנאצר מלכא דאתור ומלך סנחריב בריה תחתוהי ובהלין יומיא
סניאו אנגרייתא ולא יכיל טובי למיזל לארעא דמדי דפסקו עברי אורחא
מטול ביהלתא ולא נסב כספיה מידא דגבאל: וביומי סנחריב עבד
10 טובי זכוון סניאן לחשיכיא והוה זיין כפנין ויתמין ומלביש ערטילאין
והוה גמיל חסדא סני וכד הוה חזי קטילא רמי באורחא דיהודאי הוה
קביר ליה: וכד תב סנחריב בביהות אפין מיהודה אזל לנינוה בתקוף רגז
על עשר שיבטיא דבארעא דאתור וקטל מנהון סני והות נבילתהון
רמיין באורחא ולית קביר כד חמא טובי כדין סני באיש עליה וקם
15 בליליא וגנב פגריהון וקבר יתהון וכדין עבד זימנין סגיאן: זימנא חדא
תבע סנחריב פגרי קטיליא ולא אשכח יתהון ואזלו אנשי נינוה ואכלו
קורציה למלכא דטובי דקבר יתהון פקיד מלכא למקטליה כד שמע
טובי קם וערק ופקיד מלכא למישלל ית ביתיה ואיטמר מקמיה חמשה
וארבעין יומין עד דאדרמלך ושראצר בנוהי קטלוניה בחרבא ואינון
20 אישתזבו לארע קרדו ומלך אסרחדון בריה תחותיה ומני מלכא אסרחדון
לאקיקר בר חמאל אחוהי רבא על כל דליה ושליט בכל ארעא דאתור
ומליל אקיקר מלין טבין על טובי למלכא ובעא מיניה ואתבזיניה לנינוה.
מטול דהוה אקיקר רחימיה וקריביה ובאנונה[1] ההיא אהדרו ליה חנה
איתתיה וטוביה בריה:

ב

והוה כד מטא חגא דשבועיא אתקין אריסטוון רב וכד יתיב
על פתורא אמ לטוביה בריה זיל ואייתי לי מאחנא מסכניא מן
דחליא דאלהא למיכל עמנא ואנא אמתין לך עד מייתך: ואזל טוביה
ואשכח גברא חד קטיל רמא באורחא וחוי לאבוהי וכד שמע
טובי כן קם מן פתורא ולא אכל ואזל ונטליה מן רחובא 5
דקרתא ואעליה בחד ביתא עד מיעל שמשא דיכיל למקבריה ותב
לביתיה ואכל לחמיה באילוא ובדוונא ואמר ווי דאיתקיים בנא
והפכתי חגיכם לאבל ובכא בכיה רבא לחדא: וכד על שימשא
אזל וקבריה וקריבוהי נחכין עלוהי ואמרין לית דין דחיל מן נפשיה
והוא קבר מיתיא: ובליליא ההוא לא טבל מן מיתא ושכב על 10
ערסיה סטר כותלא ואפוהי גליין ולא ידע דצפרין קיימין עלוהי בכותלא
ונפל מצואתהון על עינוהי והות חילוא בעיניה וכל צפר וצפר הוה אזיל
לאסייא[1] לאסאה עיניי ולא איתסי אלא אסני חיורא בעינוי עד דאיסתמי
והוה סמיא ארבע שנין וכל אחוהי וכל קריבוהי הוו עציבין עליה ואקיקר
הוה מפרנס יתיה: לימנין סגיאין חנה אתתיה הוה עבדה עבידתא 15
לנשייא חורנייתא ויהבו ליה גריא חד גריא חד בגין אגרה והוה שמע גדיא זעיק
בביתא ושאל יתה מנן ליך גריא הדין דילמא גניב הוא אהדר יתיה
למריה דלא כשר לנא למיכל מן גניבתא ענת יתיה ליתוי מן גניבתא
ברם באגר עובד ידאי קבילתיה ולא האמין טובי למילתא ונצא עמיה
על גדיא. ענת חנה אנתתיה ואמרת ליה אן מובך וזכוותך וקלנך 20
אתגלי לכולא:

ג

כד שמע טובי אתאלץ סגי ובכא ושרא לצלאה בעקת נפשיה וכדין[2]
אמר זכאי את אלהא רבא וכל עובדך גבורתא וכל אורחתך טיבו וקשוט

---

[1] MS. לאסייא.   [2] MS. וכדון.

ואת דיין כל ארעא לא תנקום מינאי כחובאי וכחובי אבהתאי ואנא
ואבהתאי חבנא קדמך ואעדינא מפקודך ויהבתה יתנא לשביא ולבזה
לקלנא ולשועי לכל עממיא דאגליתא יתנא ביניהון וכען אלהא רחמך
נפישין ודינך קשוט לא תגמול עמי כחובאי ברם כחסדך סגיא עביד
5 עמי וקביל נפשי מן ידאי ארום טב לי מותי מחיי במסכנות רבתא
ובחיסודא אלין ולא אשמע קלנא עוד : וביומא ההוא שרה בת רעואל
דהות באגבתנים מדינתא בארעא דמדי שמעת חיסודא רבתא מטול
דאתיהיבת לשבעה גוברין לאינתו ולא על עלה באורח בל ארעא
ארום אשמדאי מלכא דשידי קטיל יתהון עד לא יעלון עלה באורח כל
10 ארעא אמרת ליה אמהה אנת היא דקטלת ית גובריא דיליך מטול
דאתיהיבת לשבעה גוברין וחד מנהון לא עאל עלך דאנת מלקה יתהון
ובדיל גובריא דקטלת לואי דתימות אנת כמה דמיתו אינון ולא נחזי
מנך לא ברא ולא ברתא לעלם : והוה כד שמעת שרה מיליא אילין
אתאלצת סגי ובכת וסליקת לעיליתא דאבוהא וצבת למצלב גרמה
15 ולאחתא שיבתא דאבוהא בדוונא לשאול[1] מטול בן לית לי טב למצלב
גרמי ברם טב לי לצלאה קדם אלהא ולא אשמע חיסודא תוף : בעידנא
ההיא פריסת ידהא בצלו קדם אלהא וכדין אמרת בריך את יי' אלהים
רחמנא וחננא ובריך שם קדשך דמפרש בכל עלמיא יברכונך כל עובדי
ידך לעלם ולעלמי עלמין וכען יי' קדמך אריםית אפאי ועיניאי לוותך
20 תליין אימר דאתיב לעפרי ולא אשמע חיסודאי עוד גלי קדמך יי'
דדכיא אנא מכל סואבת גבר ולא סאיבית ית שמאי[2] וית שמא דאבא
בארע תותבותי. יחידה אנא לאבא ולית ליה בר למירת אחסנתיה ולא
קריב אית ליה די ישארינני ליה והרי מיתו בגיני שבעה גוברין ומה
אית לי תוף חיי ואם לית טב קדמך למיקטל יתי חום עלאי ולא

אשמע חיסודא תוף׃ ביומא ההוא עלת צלותא דתרויהון קדם כורסי
יקרא דאלהא רבא ושלח מלאכא רפאל לאסאה תרויהון. ית טובי
לאעדאה חיורא מעינוי וית שרה בת רעואל למיתן לטוביה בר טובי
לאינתו ולאעדאה אשמדאי מלכא דשידי מינה׃ ¹וכד שיצי טובי ית
צלותיה תב לביתיה ושרה בת רעואל נחתת מעיליתא דאבוהא כד ₅
שיציאת לצלאה׃

ד

בה בשעתא דכר טובי ית כספא דאפקיד בידא דגבאל בקורי ריגש
בארעא. דמדי ואמר בליביה הא שאלית ית נפשי ליממת איקרי ית ברי
טוביה ואודע ליה עסקא דכספא עד לא אימות׃ וקרא טוביה בריה
ואמר ליה ברי כד אימות קבר יתי ביקר וייקר ית אימך ולא תשבקינה ₁₀
כל יומי חייהא ועביד לה כל דתקין בעינהא ולא תסרב על מימר
פומהא אידכר כמה אתעיקת עלך² וכד מיתא קבר יתה עמי בקברא חד׃
וכל יומך יי׳ אלהך תדחל ולא תצבי למיחטי ולא תעבר על תפקדתייא
עביד צדקתא כל יומך ולא תהך. עם גבר חטוף ארום אם תעביד קשוט
טב לך בכל דלך וכל עבדי צדקתא טוביהון׃ ברי מנכסך עביד צדקתא ₁₅
ולא תתכסי מן גבר חסיך ואלהא לא יכסה שכינתיה מינך. ברי עד
דאית יוכלא בידך למעבד צדקתא עביד ואם מתרחק מינך עותרא
עביד צדקתא ותקנה נכסין ואם תעביד צדקתא דרופתא³ טב תקנה ביום
ריתחא ארום היא משיזבא מן מותא ולא תשבוק למרה למיחת חשוכא⁴
טבתא וכל מאן דעביד לה יתקיים בדילה הלא אבהתנא לא אישתבחו⁵ ₂₀
אילהן בצדקתא באברהם אבונא כתבא מפרש כי ידעתיו למען אשר
יצוה את בניו ואת ביתו אחריו וגו לעשות צדקה ומשפט ביצחק כת

---

¹ Chapter iv in the Hebrew translation.   ² Omission.
³ For הופתק =ὑποθήκη.   ⁴ Omission.   ⁵ MS. אישתבחו.

ויזרע יצחק בארץ ההיא ביעקב כ̇ת̇ וכל אשר תתן לי עשר אעשרנו
לך : ברי מכל עצת חטאין ומכל טעותא מנע גרמך וסב לך אתתא
מזרעיתך ולא תיסב מן בני עממיא ארום בני נביאי אנן מטול דנביאי
קדמאי הוו נח ואברהם יצחק ויעקב אבהתאנא מעלמא הוי דכיר כל

5 אילין נסיבו נשין מזרעא דאחוהון ואתבריכו בבניא וזרעייהו אחסינו
ארעא : וכען ברי רחם ית אחך ולא יזוח לבך בבניא ובבנתא *ברי הב
לבך לכל עובדך ודסאני לך לחורני לא תעביד ארום בזדונא שגושיא
אית והיא מרחק קדם יי̇[1] לא תבית אגרת אגירא עמך ופולחנך ישלם
לך אלהא מלחמך הב לכפנין וממלבושך הב לערטילאין ולא יקשה

10 בעינך : ברי לחמך וחמרך אשוד על קברי זכאין ושמע למלכא טבא
בכל עידן שאל אלהך והוא יכשר אורחותך ארום לית לאיניש מלך
טב אלהין אלהא ארום כל דצבי מרים וכל דצבי מהשפיל : ברי טר
אמרי פומי ופקודי ולא ילזון מעינך : וכען ברי אודעך עסק כספי עשר
ככרין דאפקדית בידא דגבאל בקורי ריגש במדי ארום לא ידעית יום

15 מותי : וכען קדם יי̇ תדחל ותיטר גרמך מכל חובא ובצנעה תהך עימיה
ויתן לך עותר רב :

<h1 style="text-align:center">ה</h1>

ענה טוביה לאבוהי כל דפקדתני אעביד אבל איכדין איכול למיסב
כספא מידא דגבאל דהוא לא חכים לי ואנא לא חכים ליה ומה סימנא
איהב ליה ויהימין לי ויתן לי ית כספא ואורחא דיובילני למדי לא

20 ידענא : אתיב טובי ואמר לטוביה ברי דין לך סימנא טועניה יהב לי
וטועני יהבית ליה כמה דשויתי כספא ופקדתיניה בידיה ומן יומא
ההוא עד יומא דין עשרין שנין : וכען ברי פשפש גבר מהימן מן דיהך
עמך וניהב ליה אגריה זיל ברי עד דאנא קיים וסב ית כספא : ונפק
טוביה למיבלש גבר דיהך עמיה ואשכח ית רפאל מלאכא קאים ולא

---

[1] Transposition and omission.

חכמיה דמלאכא דיי' הוא שאליה מנן את אתיביה מבני ישראל חד
מאחך אמר ליה טוביה חכים את למיזל למדי אמ' ליה מלאכא ידענא
אורחיה ובמדי הוינא אושפיזא עם[1] גבאל אחונא דיתיב באגבתנים[2] עד
ראגיש והיא בנויה בטורא ואגבתנים במישרא אמ' ליה טוביה אמתין
לי ציבחר ואחוי לאבא דרגיג אנא דתהך עמי ואתן לך אגר אורחא 5
אמ' ליה אנא עכיבנא עד דתיתי : אזל טוביה וחוי לאבוהי אשכחית
גבר חד מאחנא דיהך עמי נם ליה טובי זיל קרא ליה ואידע מאידין
שבטא הוא אם מהימן הוא למיהך עמך נפק טוביה וקרא ליה ואזל
רפאל לטובי ואמר ליה שלם עלך אמר טובי ואית שלם עלי למה אירע
לי כל דא ואנא לא חזינא נהורא דשמיא קל מלין אנא שמע וגברא 10
לא חזינא ואנא שכיב בחשוכא אמר רפאל יכיל אלהא לאסאה עינך
ארום גבר חסידא את : אמר ליה טובי טוביה ברי צבי למהך למדי את
יכיל למהך עמיה וניתן אגרך אמר ליה יבילנא גברא שליחא אנא
וחכימנא שביליא ותחומיא. וטוריא ידענא : אמר טובי חוי לי מאידין
שבטא את ושום קרתא דאת דייר בה אמר רפאל אם לית אנא בשר 15
בעינך זיל ובליש גברא חורנא דיהך עם ברך אמ' ליה טובי אחי לא
תכעום עלי דצבינא למידע בקושטא ית שמך ומאידין זרעיתא את אמר
ליה אנא עזריה בר חננאל מביתא דשלמיה רבה מאחך ואמר טובי
בהשקט ובשליוותא תיתי אחי לא תרגז עלי על דבעינא למידע זרעיתא
דילך והא אחי מזרעיתא טבא הוא ואנא חכמית חננאל ונתן תרין בני 20
דשלמיה רבא והון סלקין עמי לירושלם כד יתיבנא בארעא דישראל
וסגדין עמי תמן ולא שנו אילין באנונא דטעו אחנא מזרעיתא טבתא
את עול בשלם ואתן לך אגרך טרפעיקא כל יומא ומיכלך שוה לברי
ותוף אטפי על אגרך : ענא רפאל לא תדחל דאנא אהך עם ברך וניתוב

---

[1] MS. נם.   [2] Omission.

בשלם: קרא טובי לטוביה בריה נם ליה ברי אתקין גרמך ופוק לאורחא
עם אחך אלהא דשמיא ידבר יתכון לתמן לשלם וישלח מלאכיה עמכון
ויצלח אורחכון ויתיבכון לשלם: נשק טובי[ה] לאבוה ולאמיה ואמרו ליה
זיל לשלם ונפקו למהך ובכת אמיה ואמרת לטובי מטול מנא לא
5 דחילתא למשלח טליא ארום בר יחידאי הוא לנא והוא יפוק וייעול
קדמנא בלא כספא פרנסנא אלהא אמר לה טובי לא תדחלין בשלם
ייזיל ובשלם יתוב ומלאך טב ייזיל עמיה ויצלח אורחיה ועינך תחזון
יתיה דיתוב בשלם ומנעי מלמבכי:

ו

אזל טליא ורפאל עמיה ואתו עד נחל תיגרין ברמשא ובתו תמן
10 ורהט טוביה לנהרא למשונא רגלוי ובשלו נפק נון חד מן נהרא ואכל
לחמא דטליא וצווח טליא אמר ליה רפאל אחיד נונא ולא תשבקיניה
ותפש ית נונא ואפקיה ליבשתא אמר ליה רפאל בזע נונא במציע וסב
ליביה הוא טב לאקטרא מיניה קדם נברא דאית ביה רוח שידא ורוחא
בישתא וייערקון מניה ומררתא למימשח מיניה עיינין דאית בהון חיורא
15 ויתסון: עבד בן טוביה ונסב ליבא ומררתא ונונא אפה ואכל ומותרא
שבק באורחא ואזלו עד מדי ואתו באגבתנים ואמר רפאל לטוביה אחי
עם רעואל תיתי דהוא נבר סב. וליה ברתא חדא שפירתא לחדא ושמה
שרה ואימר ליה דיתנינה לך לאנתו והיא יחידה לאבוהא והוא רחים
לה. טובא והיא איתתא טבתא ודחלת שמיא וכד נתוב מן ראניש
20 נעביד חופתא וידענא ארום לא יסרב רעואל פומך ויתן יתה לך
ונובלינה עמנא לאבוך: אמר טוביה לרפאל שמעית דהיא אתיהיבת
לשבעה גברין ומיתו עד לא עלו לוותה ושמעית דאשמדאי מלכא דשידי
קטיל יתהון ובען אנא דחיל מן שידא דילמא יקטלינני ואחית שיבתא דאבא
[ואמא] בדוונא לשאול ולית להון בר חורן ולא ברתא למקבריננ במותהון:

אמר ליה רפאל אית את דכיר תפקדתא דאבוך דפקדך דתסב אתתא
מזרעיתא דאבוך ובען קביל מני ולא תדחל מן שידא ידענא דתסבינה
ליליא הדין לאיתתו וכד תיעול באנדרונא עמה סיב ליבא דנונא ואקטר
מיניה תחות לבושא ושידא מורח והוא עריק ולא יתוב לעלם וכד תצבי
למיעל לותה קומו מן ערסא . וצלו ובעו רחמין מן קדם אלהא דאפקיד   5
עליכון טיבוותיה ויתן לך אסותא ובכן תיעול לותה ותוליד מינה בנין
לא תדחל ארום לך הות מחזיא מיומא דעלמא ואת תפרקינה מן
שידא : כד שמע טוביה מיליא האילין עלת רחימתא דשרה בלביה :

ז

ועלו בבית רעואל באגבתנים ואשכחו יתיה סטר תרע ביתיה ושאילו
בשלמיה אמר להון עולו בשלם לביתא ועלו לביתא אמר רעואל לעדנה   10
אתתיה כמה דמי הדין טליא לדמותא דטובי אחי שאילת להון עדנה מנן
אתון אתיבו לה מן שביתא דבנינוה משיבטא דנפתלי אמרת להון הידעתון
טובי אחונא אמרו לה ידענא דשלם ליה אמר טוביה טובי אבא הוא
רהט רעואל לקדמותיה וגפיף ליה ונשיק ליה ובכו : אמר רעואל בריך
טובי ואת בר זכאי וקשיט ורפיונא דידיא הוא לנשי חיסדא על דאתעוור   15
גבר זכאי ועביד זכוותא ומצוותא סגיאן וגפיף רעואל לטוביה בר אחוהי
ובכא על צואריה ועדנה אנתתיה ושרה ברתיה בכו עלוהי : נכס רעואל
דיכרא חד ואתקינו להון שירו ואכלו ושתו עד לא אכלו אמר טוביה
לרפאל מליל עם רעואל על שרה ברתיה ויתנינה לי לאינתו : מליל
רפאל עם רעואל פתגמי טוביה אתיב רעואל לטוביה ברי ידענא טב   20
דאתן יתה לך מדאתן יתה לגבר חורן ברם אמרנא לך קושטא כבר
יהבית יתה לשבעה גברין וכלהון מיתו עד לא עלו לותה ובען אכול
ושתי אמר טוביה לא איכול עד דתיתנינה לי : אמר רעואל סב כען יתה
ארום את אחוהא והיא אחתך ובען יהיבה לך לאנתו כהלכת אוריתא

דמשה יי׳ אלהא דשמיא יפרוקינכון בליליא דין ויפקיד עליכון טיבותיה

ושלמיה : ודבר רעואל ית שרה ברתיה ויהב יתה לטוביה לאנתו אמר

ליה סיב יתה כהלכת אוריתא דמשה ודבר יתה לאבוך : וקרא רעואל

לעדנה אתתיה לאיתאה נייירא למכתב עלוהי כתובתא לברתיה ועבדת

5 כן וכתבו כתובתא וחתמו יתה סהדין ואכלו ושתו : אמר רעואל לעדנה

אנתתיה אתקיני אידרון בית משכבא ואעלי ברתך ועבדת כן ונפיפת

עדנה לשרה ברתה ובכת ואמרת ברתי יעביד עמך אלהא דשמיא

בליליא הדין חיסדא וישגח עליכי ויתן לך חדווא על דוונא דהוו לך

בעידנין דעברו :

ח

10   והוה כד שלימו לאתקנא אידרונא וערסא ועלו לתמן טוביה ושרה

אנתתיה ודבר טוביה מלוי רפאל ונסיב ליבא דנונא ושוי על מחתה

וקטר תחות גלימת שרה ואשמדאי קביל ריחא וערק בסייפי ארעא

דמצרים ורפאל קטריה ואסריה לתמן : ונפקו מן אידרונא ואחדו דשא

בדיל תרויהון וקם טוביה מן ערסא ואמר לשרה אחתי קומי ונירמי

15   תחננא קדם אלהא דיפקיד עלנא חיסדיה וטיבותיה וצלי טוביה קדם

אלהא ואמר בריך את יי׳ אלהיה דישראל ובריך שמך לעולם יברכונך

שמיא וכל בריותך את בריתא אדם ויהבת ליה סמ[ך] ית חוה

אתתיה ומינהון כל בני אינשא ואמרת לא תקין למיהוי אדם בלחודוהי

אעביד ליה סמך לקבליה וכען אלהא את ידעת ארום לא בדיל זנותא

20   נסבית אחתי דא אלהין כהלכת אוריתא חוס עלנא והב לנא חסדך

לאתחברא אך חדא בשלם והב לנא בנין טבין ואתיבת שרה ואמרת

אמן : ועל לוותה בליליא הוא והות בפילגות ליליא קם רעואל ואמר

לעבדוהי לחפרא קברא בליליא ואמר להון אם מית טליא נקברניה

בליליא ואינש לא ידע ולא יהא לנא חיסודא וקרא לעדנה אנתתיה

25   ואמר לה שדרי חדא מן אמתין לאידרונא דבוצינא בידה ותחזי אם

הוא קיים ואם לא ונקבריניה ואיניש לא ירגיש : ושלחת עדנה אמתה
לאידרונא וחזת והא שכבין תרויהון ונפקת ואמרת להון בריכו מרי
עלמא ארום קיים הוא : ואמר רעואל בריך את יי׳ אלהא דשמיא וארעא
את מחי ומסי וברכתך קדישא ודכיא יברכונך חסידך וכל יציר ידך
5 ומלאכך יודונך לעולם ובריך שום יקרך ארום יהבת לנא חדותא
בסגיאות טיבותך ולא כמה דאנן חשבין בריך את אלהא ארום חסתא
על תרויהון הב להון שלמא וחסדא וחדוה בחייהון לעלם : ואתו עבדוהי
ואמר להון כסיאו ית קברא עד לא ירגיש בנא בר נש ואמר לאנתתיה
אתקיני לחם סגי ורהוטי לעדרא וסיבי מתמן עגלין וערבין ופקידי
10 למעבד אריסטוון טב ועבדת כן : ואמר לטוביה לא תפוק מן ביתי עד
ארבסר יומין ותחדי ברתי עגינתא ותיסב פלגות ניכסאי כען וכד נמות
אנא ואנתתי תיסב כולא את תהא לי לבר יקיר ואנא אהא לך לאבא
ועדנה אנתתי לאימא עד עלם :

ט

בכן קרא טוביה לרפאל ואמר ליה עזריה אחי דבר עמך מכא
15 ארבעה עבדין ותרין גמלין וזיל לראגיש סטר גבאל והב ליה מרצופיה
ויתן לך כספא וזמין יתיה לכילתי מטול דאנא לא יכילנא למיזל לתמן
בדיל דקיים רעואל דלא אפוק מן ביתיה עד ארבסר יומין ואבא מני
יומיא ואם יעבר עדנא יומא חד אציף נפשא דאבא ולא יכילנא
לבטלא קיים רעואל : אזל רפאל עם תרין גמלין וארבעה עבדין
20 לקורי ראגיש ובתו בביתא דנבאל ויהב ליה מרצופיה וחוי ליה דטוביה
בר טובי נסב שרה בת רעואל וטוביה הוה זמין ליה דייזיל לחופתיה
כד שמע גבאל כן טען כספא על גמליא ואתא לכילתא ואשכח טוביה
יתיב על פתורא ונשק ליה ובכא עלוהי מסגיאות חדואתא וברכיה
ואמר אלהא דשמיא יברך גבר טב וקשיט עביד צדקתא סגיא ובריך
25 אלהיה דטובי קריבי דיהב לך ולאבוך ולאמך אתתא טבתא הדא :

ף

ובכל יומא ויומא טובי חשיב יומי בריה כמה יומין יכיל למיזל
לקבלא כספא וכמה יומין למהדר וכד שלימו יומי חושבניה וטוביה
בריה לא תב אמר בנפשיה דילמא עכבוניה תמן או מית גבאל ולא
יהבו ליה כספא ושרי לאתאנאה וחנה אתתיה אמרת ליה אבד ברי

5 ולית נפשיה בחיין ועל דין הוא מתאחר ושרי למספד ולמבכי על ברה
ואמרת ווי לי ברי דשלחיתך למיזל לארע רחיקתא נהור עיניך למה
שבקתיה למיזל וטובי הוה אמר לה שתיקי לא תתבהלין יתי ברך
בשלם ברם מורע הוה ליה וגברא דאזל עמיה מהימן הוא לא תנסיסי
גרמיך ארום ייתי בשלם וחנה אמרת ליה שתוק ולא תנחמינני על ברי

10 והות נפקת לפרשת אורחיא ביממא ובליליא אתר דברה ייתי ביה ולא
טעימת מדם אילהן דמעתא בליליא ולא נח לבה: וכד שלימו ארבסר
יומי חופתא אמר טוביה לרעואל שלחנא ארום אבא ואמא לא סברין
למחזי יתי וכען במטו מינך שלח יתי דלא יכילנא לאיתעכבא תוף:
אמר ליה רעואל אוחר עמי תוף ואשגר לחוואה לאבוך כל דעבדת:

15 אתיב ליה טוביה הב לי רשו למיתב לאבא בכן קם רעואל ויהב שרה
ברתיה לטוביה ופלגות נכסיה עבדין וחמרין וגמלין עאן ותורין ולבושין
ומאנין דכסף ודהב ושלח יתהון בשלוה ובהשקם וברכינון ואמר להון
אלהא ישוי עליכון שלמא ויחזי לי מנכון בנין עד לא אימות ונפיף
להון ונשיק להון ואמר לשרה ברתיה איזהירי ביקרא דחמוך וחמותיך

20 דתרויהון קריביך זיל לשלם ונשמע מנך בשרתא טבתא וחדוא רבתא
ונשק לה ושלחה: ועדנה אמרת לטוביה ברי ואחי את אלהא דשמיא
ידבריניך בשלם ויחזיינני בנין קשיטין קדמוי מן שרה ברתי והא שרה
ברתי בידך לא תעני יתה כל יומי חייה זיל בשלם אנא אימך ושרה
אתתך אלהנא יצלח ארחיכון כל ימי חייכון ונישקת להון ושלחתנון:

25 ואזל טוביה חדי ובריך אלהא דשמיא וארעא דשלח מלאכיה ואצלח

אורחיה ובריך רעואל ועדנה אנתתיה ואמר אלהא יסעדיננני ליקרא
יתכון כל יומי חייכון:

יא

ואזל טוביה עד אקרים קרתא די קבל נינוה אמר רפאל לטוביה
אחי את ידע איכדין שבקת ית אבוך וכען תיזיל אנתתך בתרנא עם
גוברייא דילן ואנא ואת ניזיל לפנאה ביתא ואזלו תרויהון קדמאין[1]
ואשכחו אמיה יתבא בפרשת אורחיא מסכייא ית ברה וכד חזת יתיה
רהטת לקדמותיה וגפיפת ונשקת ליה ואמרת בריך אלהא דאיתיבך
בשלם דאנא לא חשיבית למיחזי אפך לעלם וכען ברי מה אוחרת
למיתי וחוי ליה כל עובדיא וחדיאת סגיא ואמרת לה[2] זיל את לאבוך
ואנא קאימנא הכא עד דתיתי אנתתך ואזל טוביה ורפאל עמיה וכד
שמע טובי ארום אתא בריה חדי סגי ואמר ליה ברי תב לותי ואנשק
לך דאנא לא יכילנא למיזל לותך: אמר ליה רפאל לטוביה סב
מררתא דנונא ושוי בעינוי ואסי אלהא ית עינוהי * ביד מן[3] אוולא וחדי
טובי על חסדא רבה דעבד עמיה אלהא ובריך טובי ית אלהא ואמר
בריך אלהא דלא מנע טיבותיה מני ואפקיננני מחשוכא לנהורא את 15
הוא מחי ומסי לית כותך אסי מגן ולית אלהא בשמיא ובארעא דיעבד
כעובדך וכגברוותך: ואשתעי טוביה לאבוי כל דעבד עמיה ביתא ונפק
טובי עם טוביה בריה לקדמות כלתיה ורפאל עמהון והוי כד חזאה
חדי עלה ואעלה לביתיה ובריך ואמר יתן אלהא לך מן אנתתא הדא
בנין קשיטין ועיני ועיני אמך חמן:

יב

וכד עלו לביתא לא על עמהון רפאל ואזל ליה: בתר שעתא אמר
טובי לטוביה פוק לשוקא וקרא עזריה אחונא וניתן ליה אגריה ועוד
נוסיף עליה ארום גבר מהימן וקשיט הוא: ונפק טוביה לשוקא ובלש

ולא אשכח לרפאל ושאל עלוי לכל אינשי קרתא ולא אשכח בר נש

די חזייה : תב לאבוי ואמר ליה לא אשכחתיה וידע אבוי ארום מלאכא

רפאל הוה דשדר אלהא לאסאה שרה מידוי דשידא ולאסאה עינוי

ובריך אלהא. ואמר בריך אלהא דשלח מלאכיה טב עם ברי ואצלח

5 אורחיה ואסי תרין חסיכין מרעין¹ כותנא : ומיומא ההוא ולהלא אצלח

אלהא לטובי ולטוביה בריה ויהב ליה בנין מן שרה אנתתיה ומית

רעואל ועדנה אנתתיה וירת טוביה כל נכסיהון :

———————

בתר יומין אתמרע טובי וקרא לטוביה בריה ופקדיה על מצוותא

דאלהא ואמר לה ברי הוי גמיל חיסדא כל יומך עם חסיכי ועתירי

10 ועביד צדקתא כל יומך דבגין כן יברך אלהא כל עובדי ידך אברהם

אבונא בדיל צדקתא ומעשרא דיהב ברכיה יי' וכן יצחק על דיהב

מעשרא ועבד צדקתא וכן יעקב כד אזל לביתא דלבן וצלי צלותיה לא

נדר אלא למיהב מעשרא [ו]צדקתא לחסיכי ובכן אצלחיה אלהא ויהב

ליה כל מה דשאיל ונטריה מלבן ומעשו אחוהי ואת אם תעביד

15 כעובדיהון יברכך כמה דבריך יתהון : ופקיד יתהון על שאר מצוותא

ושלים לפקדא יתיה ואתכנש לעמיה וקבריה טוביה בריה ביקר רב

ובתר מותיה בריך אלהא לטוביה על דקיים מצוותא דאבוי ואצלחיה

סגי ויהב ברכתא בכל עובדי ידוי :

———————

הא למדנו כמה גדול כח הצדקות והמעשרות על שעשה טובי

20 צדקות והפריש מעשרותיו כראוי מה שלם לו הקב"ה. ולפי שהיו יודעין

אבות העולם כח הצדקה והמעשרות לכך היו זהירין בהם. באברהם

כת ויתן לו מעשר מכל. ביצחק כת ויזרע יצחק בארץ ההיא ואין

זריעה אלא צדקה כמה דאתאמר זרעו לכם לצדקה. ביעקב כתב

וכל אשר תתן לי עשר אעשרנו לך :

✦ תם מעשה טוביה ת"ל ✦

———————

II. HEBREW TRANSLATION.

[⁘ ספר טובי ⁘]

א

זה ספר טובי בן טוביאל בן חננאל (בן אריאל) בן *גביאל בן[1]
עשאל בן ננתיאל[2] ממטה נפתלי (אשר הגלה משומרון עם הגולה אשר
הגלתה בימי הושע בן אלה) אשר הגלה בימי שלמנאסר[3] מלך אשור
והוא היה מתושבי[4] עיר נפתלי אשר בגליל על גבול ימה: ויאמר טובי
זכרה לי, אלהי לטובה (על) שהלכתי לפניך כל ימי חיי בדרך תמים 5
וצדקות רבות וחסדים טובים שעשיתי לאחי ולעמי בגולה בנינוה בארץ
אשור, ויהי בהיותי נער בארץ ישראל כל מטה נפתלי פשעו בבית דוד[5]
ויחדלו מעלות ירושלים *העיר אשר בחר יי מכל שבטי ישראל ושם
מזבח יי המקודש לכל שבטי ישראל והיכל יי בנוי בתוכה להעלות[6]
עולות ושלמים ליי שלשה פעמים (בשנה) וכל אחי[7] מטה נפתלי זובחים 10
זבחים ועולות לעגלי הזהב אשר עשה ירבעם בן נבט מלך ישראל
בבית אל ובדן ואני הלכתי אל ירושלים במועדים ככתוב בתורת יי על
ישראל בבכורים ומעשרות ובכורות לכהנים בני אהרן (ודגן ותירוש)
ושמן (ותאנים ורמונים) ומכל פרי האדמה לבני לוי המשרתים את פני
יי בירושלים ומעשר שני ומעשר שלישי לגר ליתום ולאלמנה (והלכתי 15

---

[1] P. גבריאל בר; all MSS. have גביאל almost everywhere.
[2] P. גנתיאל.   [3] P. everywhere שלמלאסר.   [4] So all; Pr. או וילאית.
[5] Pr. adds פאדשאה ישראל.   [6] P. ולהעלות.   [7] M. אישי.

בכל שנה ושנה עם כל אלה לירושלם) כמצות יי וכאשר צותה עלי
דבורה אם אבי כי יתום נשארתי (מאבי ו)מאמי. וכאשר גדלתי
לקחתי[1] אשה ממשפחתי ושמה חנה ותלד לי בן וקראתי שמו טוביה
וכאשר הגליתי מארץ נפתלי ישבתי בנינוה העיר הגדולה וכל אחי
5 וקרובי אוכלים לחם הגוים ואנכי לא נגאלתי בפתבגם מפני יראת יי[2]
וזכרתי את יי בכל לבי[3] ובכל נפשי[4] ויתן לי האלהים חן וחסד בעיני
שלמנאסר מלך אשור *ויפקד[5] אתי על כל אשר לו עד יום מותו
והפקדתי ביד[6] גביאל אחי אשר בארץ מדי במדינת רגאש[7] עשר
ככרי[8] כסף. ויהי כאשר מת שלמנאסר מלך אשור וימלך סנחריב בנו
10 תחתיו ויסגרו דרכי מדי מפני המלחמות אשר היו בארץ ולא יכלתי
ללכת אל ארץ מדי לקחת[9] את כספי (ואחרי כן) עשיתי צדקות רבות *לעניי
עמי מיתומים[10] ואלמנות וכאשר ראיתי חללי עמי מושלכים מחוץ לחומת
נינוה לא שקטתי ולא נחתי עד אשר קברתים . ויהי כאשר שב סנחריב
מלך אשור מיהודה אל נינוה בבשת פנים על אשר נגפו יי אלהי ישראל
15 *בארץ יהודה[11] על החרפה אשר חרף ונדף את אלהי ישראל [ועל זאת קצף
על כל קהלות ישראל אשר בכל מלכותו] ויהרג מהם הרבה מאד ואני
בקשתי לדעת דבר אמת על מה בא הגזרה הזאת על שבטי ישראל
כי ידעתי באמת *כי הק׳ב׳ה[12] אל אמונה ואין עול ומצאתי[13] שלא שמו
שבטי ישראל על לבם השמדת אחיהם אשר השמיד סנחריב מלך
20 אשור מבצריהם שלח באש ובחוריהם בחרב הרג ועולליהם רטש
והרותיהם בקע . ובמקום שיתאבלו וישתעננו לפני יי׳ על גזירת אחיהם

[1] M. ולקחתי.   [2] P. אלהים.   [3] P. לבבי.   [4] P. מאדי.
[5] P. ויפקוד.   [6] P. בבית.   [7] P. and Pr. everywhere רגאש.
[8] P. ככר.   [9] Π. from *, l. 7, ולקחת.   [10] P. וליתומים.   [11] Pr.
שיי׳ [12] M. בנאית (מאד) after דר זמין יהודה, l. 16. omits and has
וידעתי. [13] P. בהם.

ואשר קצף[1] עליהם היו אוכלים ושותים ושמחים *מתענגים בכלי
שיר[2] ובבכורות ובנבלים ולא נחלו על שבר יהודה בעונותינו ובעונות
אבותינו ככתוב[3] על יהודה השותים במזרקי יין וראשי שמנים ימשחו
ולא נחלו על שבר יוסף וגם על זאת היה היה קצף מאת יי על יהודה
וירושלם ויבא עליהם את מלך בבל עד השליבם מעל פניו ויגל 5
את יהודה מעל אדמתן. וכאשר ראיתי חללי ישראל מושלכים מחוץ
לחומה הייתי גונב גויותיהם וקברתים פעמים רבות ואמרתי יי אלהי
ישראל אתה צדיק על כל הבא עלינו כי אמת עשית ואנחנו הרשענו.
וכאשר בקש סנחריב מלך אשור את חללי עמי פגרי האנשים המומתים
ולא מצאם וילכו אנשי ננוה ויגידו למלך לאמר טובי עבדך אשר 10
הפקדת *על כל אשר לך הוא שולח את אנשיו[4] על כל חוצות נינוה
לבקש את חללי עמו והוא קובר אותם בסתר ולא ירא ממך. ויהי
כאשר שמע סנחריב את הדבר הזה ויחר אפו †עלי מאד ויצו לתפוש
אותי *ואת חנה אשתי[4] וטוביה בני ויבקש להרגני[5] בזעפו וכאשר נודע
לי הדבר הזה ברחתי מפניו ויצו לשלול את[4] כל אשר לי ונסתרתי 15
מפניו עד אשר צעקו עלי אלמנות ישראל ויתומיו[6] במר נפשם ובצום
ובבכי ונגע אל השמים משפטו ונשא עד שחקים ומכרהו אל ישראל
ביד שני בניו ויהרגוהו בחרב כי שאל את יועציו ולוקניו על מה קנא
הק'ב'ה על ישראל ועל ירושלם והשמיד מלאך יי את חיל פרעה[7] ואת
כל בכורי מצרים *והבחורי' אשר נתן יי להם תמיד ישועה על ידם[8] 20
ויאמרו לו חכמיו ויועציו כי אברהם אביהם של ישראל הוליך לשחוט

קצב .P[1]   ומתענגים בכל שיר .M[2]; בכל מזמור .Pr; באלאת
סרור .M. and II[3] כך כתוב .Not in II., but in Pr[4].
נבוכדנאצר .II[7]   ויתומים .II[6] מלך לתפשני ולהרגני .P. from †[5].
ואן גואנאן אנצי דאר בוראי באישאן המישה בובתינארי .So all; Pr[8]
אבר אישאן (עליהם?).

את בנו אולי יתרצה בו לפני יי אלהיו על כך קנא על בניו ויעש

בעבדיך נקמה. *אז אמר המלך¹ אני אשחט את² שני בני *בעבור יי³ אולי

אתרצה בם להם⁴ ויעזרני ויגע הדבר לאדרמלך ושראצר בניו ויארבו לו

ויהרגוהו (בחרב בשעה שנכנס להתפלל לפני דגון טעותו) שנאמר

5 ואדרמלך ושראצר בניו הכוהו בחרב והמה נמלטו ארץ אררט ויהי כי

מת סנחריב מלך אשור וימלוך אסרחדון בנו תחתיו ויפקד אסרחדון את

אקיקר בן חננאל אחי על כל אשר לו ומושל בכל ארץ אשור וידבר

אקיקר עלי אל המלך דברים טובים עד אשר השיבני לנינוה כי היה

אקיקר אהובי וקרובי וישיבו לי את חנה אשתי ואת טוביה בני כי צוה

10 המלך אשור לתפשם בזעפו אשר זעף עלי⁵:

ב

ובשנה ההיא בחג השבועות הכינותי [בביתי] סעודה גדולה וישבתי

על שלחני⁶ לאכול ואמרתי לטוביה בני לך והבא לנו⁷ מאחינו העניים

לאכול עמנו⁸ ואני וכל היושבים עמי לא נאכל עד בואך. וילך טוביה

בני לבקש מהעניים וישב מר נפש ויאמר אלי אבי מאחינו נהרג

15 והושלך ברחוב העיר. וכאשר שמעתי נבהלתי ויצר לי מאד ועזבתי את

שלחני והלכתי והרימותיו מן הרחוב ושמתיו ברשותי עד בא השמש

שאוכל לקברו ושבתי לביתי ואכלתי לחמי בדמעה ובקינה וזכרתי את

הדבר אשר דבר עמוס [הנביא] *בבית אל⁹ לאמר והפכתי חגיכם

לאבל וגו' ואבכה הרבה מאד. ויהי כבוא השמש הלכתי וקברתי את

20 החלל וקרובי ומשפחתי מלעיגים עלי לאמר אין זה ירא על נפשו

---

¹ בעבור ה' II.   ² Not in II., but in Pr.   ³ Pr. omits.
⁴ So all, לאלהים P.? Pr. omits.   ⁵ P. עלינו.   ⁶ P. השלחן;
⁷ II. לי.   ⁸ M. and II. continue ואמרתי, מגלם מן באן מן Pr. l. 16
⁹ P. בביתו.   וגופתם בטוביה Pr.; לטוביה

והוא¹ קובר את החללים. ובלילה ההוא אחרי קברי² את המת עשיתי
טבילה ולא יכלתי לטהר את עצמי בארץ טמאה כראוי בארץ ישראל
וכאשר דבר עלינו ירמיה הנביא לאמר לא תטהרי אחרי מתי עוד
והלכתי ושכבתי אצל הקיר ופני מגלים ולא ידעתי כי צפרים *עלי
בקיר³ ונפלה צואתם על עיני ונעשית⁴ תבלול בעיני והלכתי בבקר אל   5
הרופאים לרפאת אותי ולא יכלו והייתי עור ארבע שנים וכל אחי
וקרובי עצבים על עורות עיני ואקיקר קרובי רועה אותי. ובעת ההיא
הנה אשתי עושה מלאכה לנשים ואורגת יריעות לאחרים ומקבלת
שכרה ויהי היום ויתנו לה גדי אחד בשכרה ואשמע קול הגדי צועק
ואומר לה מאין בא הגדי הזה. השמרי בנפשך שלא יהיה גנוב. ותאמר   10
אלי לא כן הדבר כי נתון אלי על שכרי ולא האמנתי לה וצעקתי עליה
לאמר לכי ושלמי אותו לבעליו והיינו מתקוטטים יחד על עסק הגדי.
ותען חנה ותאמר אלי איה חסדיך וצדקותיך שלא יועילו לך בעת
צרתך וחרפתך מודעת לבריות:

ג

ואני נתעצבתי ונהייתי ונחלתי על שברי והתפללתי לפני יי ואמרתי   15
צדיק אתה יי וישר משפטך כי בכל מעשיך גבורה וכל דרכיך חסד
ואמת ואתה שופט הארץ ואתה צדיק על כל הבא עלי⁵ כי אמת עשית
ואני הרשעתי ועתה [יי] אב הרחמים אדון הסליחות זכרני⁶ נא [ופקדני
נא] במדת רחמיך וחסדיך ואל נא תגמול עלי כחטאתי וכעונותי
וכעונות אבותי אשר לא שמרו מצותיך וישליכו את תורתך אחרי גום   20
ותתן אותנו לחרפה ולמשל ולשנינה (בכל העמים ולמשול בנו גוים

<hr>

¹ P. שהוא.　　² M. קברתי; II. for the two words קבר.
³ P. כי בננשכאן אשיאנה שאן בוד בדיואר באלין סר מן Pr.; על הקיר.
⁴ P. ונעשה.　　⁵ P. עלינו.　　⁶ M. and II. זכר.　　(קן צפרים?)

אשר הדחתנו שם) כיום הזה ולולי יי צבאות שהותיר לנו שריד כמעט

כסדום היינו לעמורה דמינו ועתה יי (רבים . משפטיך ואמת ואל

תגמלני כעונותי וכעונות אבותי כי חטאנו לפניך ולא הלכנו בדרכיך

ועתה כטוב וכישר בעיניך עשה נא עמי ו)קח נא[1] את נפשי ממני כי

5   טוב מותי מחיי ולא אשמע חרפתי עוד. וביום ההוא נקרה[2] לשרה

בת רעואל שהיתה באגבתנים[3] במדינת ארץ מדי בעת היו משפחות[4]

אביה מחרפים אותה (ומלעיגים בה ואומרים לה לא יש ראוי לקרא לך

שרה אלא צרה)[5] על דבר *שנתנה לאשה לשבעה[6] אנשים ולא קרב לה

אחד מהם כי אם אשמדי[7] מלך השדים היה הורג אותם קודם שקרבו[8]

10   אליה כדרך כל הארץ ותאמר אליה השפחה למה את הורגת[9] את

אנשיך ותלקי אותנו על הדבר הרע הזה וטוב יהיה לאבותי שתמותי

תחתם ולא יראו ממך לא בן ולא בת לעולם. ויהי כאשר שמעה שרה

החרפה הזאת ותתחלחל מאד ותבך ותעל אל עלית אביה ותזעק לפני

יי בקול מר ותאמר יי אלהים אתה נתתני לאבי והם זקנים באים בימים

15   ואתה השלחת על אנשי׳ הלוקחים אותי את מלך[10] השדים כי אתה אלהי

(כל) הרוחות וכל השדים ויוצר כל הבריות ובידך כל מיני מזיקין

שבעולם ועתה יי הטוב בעיניך שאוריד את שיבת אבי ואמי ביגון

שאולה ואם יצא גזר דין מלפניך עלי כזאת הרגני נא הרוג ואל אראה

עוד ברעתי המרובה וחרפתי הגדולה ידעת יי כי טהורה אני מכל

20   טמאת אדם ולא טמאתי שמי ואת שם אבותי בארץ גלותי ואני יחידה

לאבי ולאמי ואין לו[11] בן לירש את נחלתו ולא . יש לו[11] קרוב שיורשני[12]

והנה מתו בעבורי שבעה אנשים ומה יתרון לי להיות עוד בעולם ואם

---

1   Only in п.   2   M. נקרא ; Pr. אנד ; 5.   3   P. and Pr. בגבתנים.

4   M. משפחת ; Pr. קבילת.   5   п. continues מן צרורה בשביל שאת.

6   п. שנעתה לאישה.   7   P. everywhere אשמדאי.   8   M. שיקרבו.

9   M. הָרַגְתָּ.   10   п. מלאך.   11   P. לי.   12   M. שיירשני לו.

לא טוב בעיניך להמיתני הביטה וענני וחנני ולא אשמע חרפתי עוד.
בעת ההיא נשמע[ת] תפלת שניהם לפני *כסא הכבוד¹ (תפלת טובי
על עורות עיניו ותפלת שרה על שפלות אבותיה) וישלח יי את המלאך
רפאל השר הממונה, על הרפואות לרפאת את שניהם את טובי אב ²
טוביה לרפאתו מחלי עיניו ואת שרה בת רעואל לתתה לטוביה בן
טובי לאשה ולהסיר ממנה את אשמדי מלך השדים:

ד

וככלות טובי את תפלתו וישב אל ביתו ושרה בת רעואל ירדה
מעלית אביה בכלותה להתפלל אל יי. בעת ההיא זכר טובי את הכסף
אשר הפקיד ביד גביאל במדינת רגאש בארץ מדי ויאמר בלבו הנה
אנכי שואל בכל יום *את נפשי³ למות⁴ ועתה אקרא את טוביה בני
ואודיע אותו את דבר⁵ הכסף בטרם אמות. ויקרא את טובי. בנו ויאמר
אליו כאשר אמות קבור אותי בכבוד וכבד את אמך ואל תעזבנה כל
ימי חייה ואל תמרה את פיה ואל תמרר⁶ את חייה וזכור בני כמה
צרות עברו עליה בהיותך בבטנה⁷ ובמותה קבור אותה עמי בכבוד
בקבר אחד וכל ימיך זכור את בוראך ולא תחטא לפניו ולא תעבור
על מצוותי ומכל אשר יתן לך יי אל תמנע *ידך מעשות⁸ צדקה ואל
תתחבר עם אנשי חמס אל תעלים אל תעלים עיניך מעניי ישראל ואל יעלים יי
עיניו ממך בעת צרתך ואם לא תשיג ידך לעשות עושר אל תמנע
מעשות צדקה. מן הנמצא בידך ותקנה לך עושר ואוצרות כסף וזהב
(בצדק)⁹ כי לא יועילו אוצרות רשע וצדקה תציל ממות וכל המתעסק
בצדקה יחזה פני אלהים ככתוב אני בצדק אחזה פניך ועוסקים עמו מן

---

¹ M. and II. יי כבוד כסא ולפני השכינה.   ² P. and II. בן.
³ II.   ⁴ M. נפשי למות.   ⁵ II. adds מן.   ⁶ M. תמרה.
⁷ M. and II. add עליך.   ⁸ P. לעשות.   ⁹ בצדקה ? Pr. omits.

השמים¹. ואתה בני מנע את עצמך מכל טמאה ומכל זנות וקח לך
אשה ממשפחתך ולא מכל בן נכר אשר לא מזרע אבותיך הוא כי
מבני הנביאים אנחנו וזכר בני את אברהם את יצחק ואת יעקב אשר
לקחו נשים ממשפחתם ולא אבו להתחתן בבני נכר ונתברכו בבנים
5 ובנות. ואתה בני שים לבך לכל² מעשיך ואשר תשנא לנפשך לא תעשה
לאחרים ולא תלין פעלת שכיר אתך *מן היום אשר תסתכם³ עמו⁴
ופעולתך ישלם לך האלהים ומנע את עצמך משכרון ולא יאנה לך כל
און ומלחמך. תן לרעבים⁵ ומבגדיך כסה ערמים ומכל העודף עשה
ממנו צדקה ואל יקשה בעיניך. *לחמך וייגך שפוך על קברי צדיקים⁶
10 ושמע וקבל לכל מי שיתן לך עצה טובה ובכל עת שאל מאת יי והוא
יישר ארחותיך ועצתך כי אין ביד אדם שום עצה אלא בידי⁷ הב"ה
(לבד) כי כל אשר יחפוץ יעשה וזה ישפיל וזה ירים ושמור אמרי וכל
אשר צויתי עליך ואל ילוזו מעיניך וחזק ואמץ כי יי יהיה עמך לעזור
ולהועיל אם תדרשנו בכל לבבך ובכל נפשך. ועתה בני אודיעך את
15 דבר הכסף אשר היה לי ביד גביאל אחי קרובי עשר ככרי כסף במדינת
רגאש (ובארץ מדי) כי לא ידעתי⁸ את יום מותי ואתה בני אם תירא
את יי *ותשמור עצמך מכל חטא הוא⁹ יתן לך עושר גדול:

ה

ויען טוביה את אביו ויאמר כל אשר צויתני אבי כן אעשה. ועתה
אבי תן לי עצה איך אוכל לקחת את הכסף מיד גביאל כי הוא לא
20 יכירני ואנכי לא אכירהו¹⁰ ומה סימן אומר אליו לתת לי את הכסף

---

¹ M. adds הם.　² M. אל; .שכר .II　³ M. תכתבם .II ; תכתבנו.
⁴ Pr. תא באמדאד　⁵ P. לעניים.　⁶ Pr. נושת תו ויין תו בי ריז.
⁷ II. ביד.　⁸ M. and II. ידעום.　⁹ P. משמור.　אבר קברהא צדיקאן.
¹⁰ M. and II. אבירנו.　והוא . . . .

וגם הדרכים שילכו בהם למדי לא ידעתים¹. ויען טובי¹ ויאמר אל טוביה

בנו הסימן אשר תאמר לו אמתחתו נתן לי ואמתחתי² קבל מידי כאשר

שמתי את הכסף בידו היום³ עשרים שנה. ועתה לך ובקש לך אדם

שיהיה איש נאמן וילך עמך ונתן לו שכרו ולך בני בעודני חי וקח את

הכסף ויי אלהי ישראל הוא ישמרך בכל דרכיך ויתנך לחן ולחסד

ולרחמים בעיני האיש ובעיני כל רואיך וישלח אותך בכבוד ובשלום

וישיבך אלינו בשלום (בטרם אמות). ויצא טוביה לבקש אדם ללכת

עמו למדי וימצא את רפאל מלאך יי עומד לקראתו ולא ידע טוביה כי

מלאך יי (צבאות) הוא. ויאמר המלאך אל טוביה *מאין אתה בחור

ויען טוביה ויאמר [מבני ישראל אנכי ויאמר טוביה]⁴ אדני התדע ללכת 10

עמי למדי ויאמר המלאך [כן] ידעתי את הדרכים כלם ובמדי הייתי

(אושפיש)⁵ בבית גביאל אחינו היושב ברגיש⁶ *מדינת המדי⁷ ודרך שני

ימים יש מאגבתניש⁸ עד רגאיש ורגאיש [בנויה]⁹ בהר ואגבתנים

[בנויה]⁹ בשדה ויאמר לו טוביה הרף מעט בחסדך ואלך ואגיד לאבי

את הדבר כי מתאוה אני מאד שתלך עמי ואתן לך שכר הדרך ויאמר 15

לו לך מהר כי הנני עומד עד שתשוב אלי ואל תאחר. ויבא טוביה

ויגד לאביו לאמר מצאתי איש טוב מאחינו שילך עמי ויאמר טובי

קרא אותו אלי ואדע מאיזה מקום הוא ואם נאמן ללכת עמך ויצא

טוביה ויקראהו. ויבא המלאך אל טובי ויאמר לו שלום אליך איש

האלהים ויאמר טובי אם יש *עלי שלום¹⁰ ולמה מצאתני כל זאת 20

שאיני רואה בעיני¹¹ ואנכי יושב עור במחשכים ויאמר המלאך מי *שעור

---

¹ II. ידעתיך.   ² All texts ואמרתי; Pr. וגופתם.   ³ II. adds הזה.

⁴ Not in II.   ⁵ II. אושפיז.   ⁶ P. and II. באגבתנים.   ⁷ P. and II. הים.

⁸ On the margin of P. marked נ״א.   ⁹ MS. בנינוה; Pr. נשינא אן

באגבנתים שהרסתאן דריאה וראה דו רוז הסת אז אגנבתים תא רגאיש

ורגאיש דר נינוה דר כוה ואגנבתים דר נינוה דר רשת   ¹⁰ P. transposes.

¹¹ P. and II. מעיני.

אותך¹ ממאור עיניך הוא ירפאך כי צדיק אתה ויען טובי ויאמר בן

(יאמר יי) ויאמר לו טובי אחי טוביה בני מבקש ללכת אל מדי [התוכל

ללכת אל מדי] התוכל ללכת עמו ואני אתן את שכרך ויאמר המלאך

בן אוכל ואני יודע (את) הדרכים כלם וכל הגבולים הלכתי וההרים

5 ידעתי ויאמר טובי מאיזה מקום אתה ומאיזה שבט אתה ומאי זה עיר

אתה ויאמר המלאך עוד תבקש *ויש לך שכיר² שׁילך עם בנך כרצונך

ויאמר טובי אחי מבקש אני לידע את שמך ומאי זו משפחה אתה

ויאמר המלאך אני עזריה בן חננאל מבית שלומית הגדול מאחיך³.

ויאמר טובי לחיים ולשלום ועתה⁴ אחי אל תבעוס עלי על שאני מבקש

10 לדעת דבר אבות⁵ ממשפחתך⁶ והנה אתה אחי ממשפחה טובה ויקרה

וגם אתה. ידעת את חננאל ואת *נתן שני בני⁷ שלומית הגדול והם

ההולכים⁸ עמי לירושלם בשבתנו בארץ ישראל ומשתחוים עמי שם ולא

תעו אלה אחרי אלהי *נכר הארץ⁹ כאשר תעו אחינו ועתה אחי¹⁰ לך לשלום

עם בני ובשלום תבואו בעזרת האל ואני אתן את שכרך זוז בכל יום

15 ומאכלך כמו לבני ואם ישיבכם הב"ה בשלום עוד אוסיף לך על שכרך

ויאמר המלאך אל תירא כי אני אלך עם בנך ונלך לשלום ונשובה

בשלום. ויקרא טובי אל בנו (ויאמר אליו) הכן לך מה שאתה צריך

לדרך וצא עם אחיך ואל שדי הוא יוליככם לשלום וי(ו)שיבכם בשלום

וישלח מלאכו עמכם ויצליח דרביכם, וישק טוביה לאביו ולאמו ויאמרו

20 לו לך לשלום ויצאו ללכת. ותחל אמו לבכות ותאמר אל בעלה איך

לא יראת לשלוח את הנער כי בן זקונים הוא (לנו) והוא יוצא ובא¹¹

לפנינו ובלא אותו כסף יחיינו אלהינו ויאמר טובי אליה אל תראי

---

¹ P. שעורך.　　²P. על השכיר (ה.) שכיר; Pr.

³ P. מאחיו.　　⁴ M. and ה. ואתה.　　⁵ P. אמת; Pr. סבון פדראן.

⁶ ה. ממשפטיך.　　⁷ P. שני בניו.　　⁸ P. הולכים.　　⁹ P. הנכר.

¹⁰ Only in ה.　　¹¹ ה. לבא.

אחותי כי בשלום ילך ובשלום [1] יבא אלינו ועניך תראינה אותו ויי
אלהינו ישלח מלאכו עמו ויצליח דרכו וישוב בשלום ותוסף *לבכות
עוד [2] :

ו

וילך הנער לדרכו והמלאך רפאל עמו ויבא [3] עד נחל תיגרין [4] בערב
וילינו שם וירד טוביה [5] אל הנחל לרחוץ רגליו. ויצא פתאום דג אחד 5
מן הנחל ויאכל [5] את [6] לחם [7] הנער ויצעק (ויאמר) לו המלאך תפוש [8]
הדג ואל תניחהו ויתפש הנער את הדג ויאמר המלאך אל הנער קרע
את הדג בתוך וקח [את] הלב *ואת המרה [9] ושים אותם עמך כי
טובים הם לרפואות ויעש כן הנער ואת הדג בשל ואכל [10] והנותר הניח.
וילכו עד מדי ויאמר טוביה אל המלאך עזריה אחי מה רפואה תעשה 10
מלב הדג והמרה [11]. ויאמר אליו הלב יועיל להקטיר ממנו לפני אדם
שיש בו רוח רעה או רוח שדים וינוסו ממנו והמרה [11] תועיל למשוח
בה העינים [12] שיש בהם לובן וירפא. ויבאו לאגבתנים [13] ויאמר המלאך אל
טוביה אחי אבית רעואל נלין כי הוא איש זקן ובת יחידה יש לו
יפת מראה [14] ושמה שרה ואדבר [15] אליו שיתננה לך לאשה והיא 15
טובת שכל ואביה אהבה ועתה שמעני ודבר בעבורה וכאשר נשוב
מן ראגיש נעשה החופה ואני ידעתי כי לא ימרה האיש את פיך
ולא יתן אותה לאיש זר ותשאנה [16] כתורת משה ונוליך אותה אל
אביך ויאמר טוביה אל המלאך שמעתי אחי שכבר נתנה [17] לשבעה
אנשים ומתו טרם שיבאו [18] אליה ושמעתי שאשמדי מלך השדים הוא 20

---

[1] M. ובשלוה.　　[2] P. transposes.　　[3] II. ויבאו.　　[4] P. תיגרון.

[5] M. לאכול.　　[6] II. omits.　　[7] M. omits.　　[8] P. קח את.

[9] II. המרירה; M. והמרירה.　　[10] M. and II. ויאכל.　　[11] M. and II.

והמרירה.　　[12] M. עיני האדם.　　[13] M. באנבתנים.　　[14] P. תואר.

[15] II. ואדברה.　　[16] Only in P.　　[17] P. נשאה.　　[18] P. שבאו.

הורג אותם ועתה ירא אני מאד פן יהרגני אשמהי והורדתי את שיבת

אבותי ביגון שאולה כי אין להם בן אחר ולא בת לקברם במותם.

ויאמר אליו המלאך ירא את יי וזכר אותו וזכור מצות אביך אשר צוך

שתקח אשה ממשפחת אביך ועתה שמעני ואל תירא מן השד כי יודע

5 אני שתקח אותה הלילה הזה לאשה וכאשר תבא בחדר עמה קח את

לב הדג והקטר ממנו *תחת בגדיה[1] ויריח השד ויברח ולא ישוב אליה

לעולם וכשתרצה[2] לבא אליה[3] קומו מן המטה והתפללו והתחננו אל יי

שיצוה לכם חסדו ורפואתו וירפאה ואז תבא אליה ותוליד ממנה בנים

זכרים ואל תירא כי לך היא ראויה קודם שנברא העולם ועל ידך

10 יושיענה יי מיד השד:

ז

ויהי כשמוע טוביה כל הדברים האלה ונפשו נקשרה בנפש שרה

ויבאו באגבתנים בבית רעואל וימצאו אותו אצל שער ביתו וישאלו לו

לשלום וישב להם שלום. [ויאמר להם באו בשלום אל הבית ויבאו

הביתה] ויאמר רעואל אל עדנה אשתו כמה דומה זה הבחור לדמות

15 טובי אחי ותשאל להם עדנה מאין אתם אחי ויענו אליה מן השביה

אשר בנינוה ממטה נפתלי ותאמר להם הידעתם את טובי אחינו ויאמרו

ידענו ותאמר להם השלום לו ויאמרו שלום ויאמר טוביה טובי אחיכם

אשר אמרתם אבי הוא. וירץ רעואל לקראתו ויחבק לו וינשק לו ויבך

עמו ויאמר רעואל ברוך אתה בני ליי כי בן איש צדיק וישר אתה

20 ויוסיפו עוד לבכות עמו רעואל ועדנה אשתו ושרה בתו וישחט איל

אחד ויכינו סעודה [בלב שמח] ויאכלו וישתו. ויאמר טוביה אל המלאך

דבר עם רעואל על דבר שרה בתו ויתננה לי לאשה ויהי כאשר שמע

רעואל הדבר הזה ויאמר אל טוביה ידעתי [בני] כי טוב תתי אותה

---

[1] Pr. אן נֶאֱמָהָא וֹיֵר.   [2] M. and II. וכאשר שתרצה.   [3] II. omits.

לך מתתי אותה לאיש אחר אבל אומר לך האמת [בני] דע כי כבר

נתתי אותה לשבעה אנשים וכלם מתו טרם שיבאו אליה ועתה אכול

ושתה והנח הדבר. ויאמר טוביה לא אכל ולא אשתה עד *אשר

תתננה[1] לי לאשה. ויאמר רעואל קח אותה כי היא אחותך ואתה אחיה

הנה נתתיה לך לאשה כדת משה וישראל ויי אלהי השמים יושיבכם 5

הלילה הזה בשלום ויצוה עליכם חסדו [ושלומו]. ויקח רעואל את שרה

בתו ויתן אותה לטוביה לאשה ויברכם ויאמר לעדנה אשתו להביא

אליו גליון אחד ויכתב עליו את הכתובה ויחתם אותה בעדים ויאכלו

וישתו וישמחו. ויאמר רעואל אל עדנה אשתו הכיני החדר *ושימי

אותם[2] שמה ותחבק עדנה את שרה בתה ותבך עמה ותאמר לה בתי 10

יי אלהי ישראל יעשה עמך חסדו בלילה הזה ויתן לכם רחמים וירחם

אתך בשביל היגון שעבר עליך[3] עד היום הזה:

ח

ויהי כאשר כלו לתקן את החדר ואת המטה ויקומו וילכו לחדר

טוביה ושרה ויזכר טוביה את דברי רפאל ויקח את לב הדג וישם על

המחתה ויקטר ויקח תחת בגדי שרה וקבל אשמדי את הריח [ויצא ממנה] ויברח 15

(עד קצה ארץ מצרים ורפאל המלאך אסרהו שם *ויצא מן החדר) ויסגרו[4]

הדלת בעד[5] שניהם. ויקם טוביה מן המטה ויאמר לשרה אשתו אחותי

קומי ונפלי תחננתנו לפני המקום שיעשה עמנו כרוב רחמיו וחסדיו ויחל

טוביה את פני יי ויאמר טוביה יי אלהי ישראל אתה הוא יי לבדך

בשמים ובארץ ואתה בראת את אדם ונתת לו את חוה אשתו לעזר 20

כנגדו ועתה אתה יי גלוי וידוע לפניך שלא לקחתי את האשה הזאת בשביל

---

[1] P. שתתננה. [2] P. ושימו אותה. [3] P. לפניך. [4] P. ויסגר;

[5] II. בעדם. ובירון אמד אזאן חוגרה ובי בסתנד Pr.

זנות כי אם ביושר לבב כדת משה וישראל ואתה יי חננו ורחם עלינו
והחבירנו יחד בשלום ותן לנו בנים לברכה ועוסקים בתורתך ותען שרה
ותאמר אמן. ויבא אליה בלילה ההוא[1] ויקם רעואל לילה ויאמר אל
עבדיו לחפר קבר לילה ויאמר אם מת הבחור נקברנו בלילה ואיש אל
5 ידע ולא יהיה לנו חרפה ויקרא רעואל אל עדנה אשתו ויאמר אליה
שלחי אחת מן השפחות אל החדר ותראה אם הוא חי ואם לא נקברהו
טרם[2] אור הבקר ואיש לא ידע. ותשלח עדנה את השפחה אל החדר
ותרא[3] והנה שוכבים שניהם יחד בשלום וחדוה ותצא ותגד להם (ותאמר
להם) כי הוא ויברכו את יי האלהים הגדול ויאמר רעואל ברוך אתה יי
10 אלהי אבותינו אשר עשית עמנו החסד הגדול הזה כי אתה הוא יי
[ה]מוחץ ו[ה]רופא [ה]ממית ו[ה]מחיה אשר עשית עם שני אלה
הפלא[4] הזה[5] ואתה חי וקים לעד[6] ולנצח נצחים ויאמר רעואל אל
עבדיו *כסו את הקבר בטרם הבקר שלא ידע אדם ויצו להכין[7] סעודה
טובה בשמחה כי שמחם[8] אלהים ברוב[9] רחמיו וחסדיו. ואל העדרים רץ
15 רעואל ויבא עגלים ואילים ויצו לעשות אותם ויאמר אל טוביה לא תצא
מביתי עד ארבעה עשר ימים[10] ושמח את בתי העגונה[11] ותקח חצי
*מכל אשר לי[12] ותלך אל אביך בשמחה וכשאמות[13] אני ואשתי תקח
את הכל :

ט

אז קרא טוביה אל רפאל[14] ויאמר לו עזריה אחי קח עמך מזה
20 ארבעה עבדים ושני גמלים ולך בא אל אל דנאיש אל גביאל דודי ותן לו
את אמתחתו ויתן לך את הכסף וקרא אותו שיבוא[15] לחופתי כי אני

---

[1] M. הוא.   [2] P. בטרם.   [3] P. ונרה בידיה.   [4] P. הפלאה.
[5] P. and II. הזאת.   [6] M. and II. לעדי עד.   [7] P. הכינו.
[8] P. שמחנו; Pr. אן פאי   [9] P. בטוב.   [10] II. יום.   [11] M. ענונה.
[12] P. בסתה.   [13] P. ובמות.   [14] P. עזריאה.   [15] P. שיבואו כלם.   [12] P. ממוני.

לא אוכל ללכת שם מפני השבועה שנשבע רעואל עלי שלא אצא [1]
מביתו עד ארבעה עשר ימים ואבי ואמי (י)ספרו את הימים ואם יעבר
הזמן יום אחד אכאיב נפש אבותי. ויקם [2] רפאל ויקח שני גמלים
וארבעה עבדים [3] וילך אל רנאיש לבית [4] גביאל ויתן לו את אמתחתו *
ויגד לו כי כי טוביה בן טובי לקח את שרה בת רעואל ויקראהו [רפאל] 5
לבא *לחפת טוביה [5] ויעמס גביאל את הכסף על הגמלים ויבא לחפתו [6]
וימצא את טוביה יושב על השלחן ויחבק לו וינשק לו ויבך עמו מרוב
השמחה ויברכהו ויאמר ברוך יי אלהי ישראל אשר החבירך בשמחה עם
*האשה והוא [7] ברחמיו יתן לך ממנה בנים זכרים ועוסקים בתורת יי :

י

וטובי ואשתו מחשבים את. הימים ואת הלילות וכואבים על אשר 10
שלחוהו ובוכים ומתענגים עליו וטובי מנחם את חנה אשתו לאמר החרישי
כי בשלום יבא ובשמחה ותמאן להתנחם ותצא [8] אל הדרכים בכל יום
לראות אם יבא בנה ולא טעמה מאומה כי אם דמעות ימים ולילות
*ויהי כאשר [9] תמו ארבעה עשר ימי החפה ויאמר [10] טוביה אל רעואל [11]
שלחני כי אבי ואמי מחשבים [12] את הימים ואינם חושבים [לראותי] ויאמר 15
רעואל שבה עוד עמדי ואשלח [13] להגיד לאביך את כל אשר עשית
ויאמר טוביה אל תאחר אותי שלחני *ואלכה אל אבי. אז נתן רעואל
את שרה בתו לטוביה וחצי ממונו [14] ועבדים ושפחות וצאן ובקר וחמורים
וגמלים ובגדי בוץ וארגמן וכלי * כסף וזהב [15] וישלחם ויברכם ויאמר

[1] M. אבא.   [2] P. וילך.   [3] P. ועברים.   [4] P. אל בית.   [5] M. and
ח. האיש ההוא (הוא) .M [7]   .לחופתה ח; לחופה .M [6]   .לחפתו ח
[8] P. וויצאה.   [9] P. וכאשר.   [10] P. בא.   [11] P. continues ויאמר לו.
[12] P. מספרים.   [13] M. and ח. ואני אשלח.   [14] M. and ח. ואלך
לאבי ולאמי וישמע רעואל בקול טוביה ויתן לו את שרה בתו וחצי עשרו
[15] P. וזהב.

(אלהים) יי אלהי אבותינו יברך אתכם ויראני מכם בנים זכרים

(ו)עוסקים בתורת יי וינשק להם ויחבק להם ויאמר אל שרה בתו כבדי

מאד את חותנך ואת חותנתך¹ ולכי לשלום ונשמע ממך שמועה טובה

בחיינו בששון ובשמחה (וישק להם ויחבקם) וישלחֵם ויאמר אל טוביה

5 בני² (יי) אלהי השמים יוליכך בשלום ויראני ממך ומשרה בתי בנים

טובים לפני יי בטרם אמות והנה שרה בתי בידך אל תענה אותה³ כל

ימיך ולכו לשלום ויברכם⁴ וישק להם וישלחם:

יא

וילך טוביה שמח וטוב לב ויברך את יי אשר שמחהו ואשר עשה

עמו נפלאות רבות וחסדים טובים וילך ויבא (אל) אקרים⁵ העיר⁶ אשר

10 נכח נינוה ויאמר רפאל [טוביה] אחי אתה ידעת איך עזבת את אביך

ואת אמך ועתה נתקדם אני ואתה *ותלך אשתך⁷ אחרינו [ו]עם

העבדים ועם אנשינו וילכו שניהם ויאמר רפאל אל טוביה קח

עמך (מ)מרירת הדג [ויקחה]. והנה אמו יושבת על הדרך לראות אם

יבא בנה ותרא[ה] אותו מרחוק ותכירהו ותאמר אל טובי אישה הנה

15 בני טוביה בא ו(ה)איש אשר הלך עמו ויאמר רפאל אל טוביה ידעתי

כי עור אביך⁸ ובמרירה הזאת יפתחו⁹ עיניו וירפא. ותרץ חנה אמו

לקראתו ותפל על צואריו [ותאמר אמותה הפעם אחרי ראותי את פניך

ותבך על צואריו עוד. (ויקם טובי וילך לקראת בנו ויכשל בלכתו כי

לא ראה) וירץ טוביה אל אביו וישם את המרירה על עיניו [ויתבררו

20 עיניו ויפול הלובן מעיניו ונתרפא וירא את בנו ויפל על צואריו ויאמר

ברוך יי אלהי ישראל אשר¹⁰ הוא פוקח עורים כי [הוא] פקח את עיני

---

¹ P. חמותך. ² P. אחי. ³ Only II. ⁴ P. ולברכה. ⁵ Pr. אקדים.

⁶ P. לעיר. ⁷ M. ואשתך תלך. ⁸ P. הוא. ⁹ P. יפקחו. ¹⁰ P. כי.

ברוך הוא וברוך שמו לעדי עד ולנצח נצחים אשר עשה עמי החסד
הגדול הזה כי הוא מוחץ ורופא וממית ומחיה (ו)ברוך הוא ומבורך
אשר הצליח דרכיך * ואשר השיבך אלינו בשלום ובשלוה¹. ויצא טובי
וחנה אשתו לקראת שרה (בת רעואל) כלתם וישמחו עמה שמחה
גדולה ויפלא מאד בעיני כל הרואים והשומעים כי נרפאו * עיני טובי² 5
ויברך טובי את שרה כלתו ויאמר ברוכה את ליי וברוך בתי אשר
הביאך אלינו בשמחה וישמחו שמחה גדולה הם וכל (ה)יהודים אשר
בנינוה על החסד הגדול הזה אשר עשה יי עם טובי ועם בנו ויתנו
לטוביה³ מתנות רבות ויקרות:

יב

ויאמר טובי אל טוביה בנו בני האיש אשר הלך עמך נתן לו שכרו 10
ועוד נוסיף עליו ויאמר טוביה אבי נתן לו [את] חצי הכסף אשר
הבאתי משם כי הוא הוליכני בשלום והביאני בשלום ורפא את אשתי
והוציא את הכסף מיד גביאל ורפא את עיניך ומה ראוי לתת לו על
כל זאת. ויקרא⁴ טוביה אל רפאל (ויאמר לו) עזריה אחי [בא ו]קח
שכרך חצי הכסף שהבאת[י] משם [כי הוא שכרך] ולך לשלום⁵. 15
ויאמר רפאל אל טובי ואל טוביה בנו שירו ליי שיר חדש וברכו(הו)
וזמרו שמו על כל הטובה אשר עשה עמכם והרבו לפניו תפלה ותחנה
וצדקה כל ימי חייכם כי טוב לפני יי לעשות צדקה תמיד מכנוס⁶
אוצרות כסף וזהב כי צדקה תציל ממות ואני לא אחד מכם כל⁷
האמת דעו כי בעת⁸ אשר התפללת[ם] והתחננת[ם] לפני (הקדוש ברוך 20
הוא) אתה ושרה כלתך על צרת נפשכם אני העליתי תפלתכם לפני

---

¹ P. טובי מעורות עיניו.   ² P. והשיב בשלום ובשמחה אלינו.
³ P. אל טוביה.   ⁴ P. ויאמר.   ⁵ P. בשלום.   ⁶ II. מגננו; Pr.
⁷ P. כי.   ⁸ II. שעת.   או אנדר בורדן

כסא הכבוד ובעת היית קובר את המתים אני הייתי עמך [ובחג

שבועות שעזבת את שלחנך והלכת לקבור את המת אני הייתי עמך]

*ובחנך האלהים[1] בעורות עיניך כי יי[2] צדיק יבחן ובעת צרתך שלחני

יי לרפא אותך ואת שרה כלתך ואני (הוא) רפאל המלאך אחד מן

5　השרים המשרתים לפני כסא הכבוד. ויהי כשמעם את כל הדברים

האלה וייראו מאד ויפלו על פניהם ויאמר [להם] רפאל שלום לכם

אל תיראו ברכו את יי על הגדלות והנוראות האלה אשר עשה עמכם

ואני בכל אשר הייתי עמכם ראיתם אותי אוכל ושותה כי כן נדמה

בעיניכם ואני לא אכלתי ולא שתיתי ועתה כתבו לכם את כל הדברים

10　האלה בספר והיה לעד ביניכם ובין אלהיכם כל ימי חייכם והדבר[3]

הזה *לאות ועד[4] בכל דור ודור וברכו את יי והודו לזכר קדשו ועתה

שלחוני ואלך אל האלהים אשר שלחני אליכם וישלחוהו ויברכו את יי

על כל זאת ויעל מלאך יי השמימה ולא יסף להראה אל טובי ואל

טוביה בנו :

יג

בעת ההיא כתב טוביה את כל הדברים האלה בשמחה ויאמר טובי　15

ברוך יי האלהים הגדול המפליא לעשות[5] פלאיו לעמו ועבדיו והוא מוחץ

ורופא וממית ומחיה ומוריד שאול ויעל אשר פזר אותנו בין הגוים

חייבין אנו להודיע את כל הנפלאות האלה בין העמים ואתם בני

ישראל חזקו ויאמץ לבבכם ולא ירפו ידיכם כי יש שכר לפעולתכם

20　והוא [יחכה לחננכם ו]ירום לרחמכם כי אלהי משפט יי אשרי כל

*חוכי לו[6] ואתם בני הרבו צדקה תפלה ותחנה לפני רבון [כל] העולם

כי צדקה ותפלה דוחין את הגזרה שנאמר וצדקה תציל ממות. [ו]ברוך

---

[1] M. and П. ויהיה הדבר P.　　וגסה אותך יי ‖　[2] הוא P.　　[3] P.

[4] לעד ולאות P.　　[5] Only in П.　　[6] M. and P. חוסים ; П. בו.

יי אשר עשה עמי ועם אבי ועם אבותי ועם כל אשר בטח בו נסים
ונפלאות ונוראות גדולות *רבון העולמים הראנו בימינו הישועה והגאולה
בביאת הגואל ובבנין אריאל לעיני כל ישראל שנאמר בימיו תושע
יהודה וישראל וכתיב ופדויי יי ישובון וכתיב בונה ירושלם יי נדחי
ישראל יכנס[1]. ברוך יי לעולם אמן ואמן:

❖ תם ונשלם ספר טובי בן טוביאל *תהלה לאל[2] ❖

---

[1] Not in M. and Pr.   [2] Only in П.

III. ADDITION TO THE MIDRASH THANḤUMÂ, § האזינו.

❖ וכך נמצא בספר הרב ר' משה הדרשן ❖

יצרנהו כאישון עינו הק״בה נוצר לבחוניו כאדם הנוצר אישון עינו.
ומעשה באדם אחד עשיר גדול ומקובל והיתה לו בת אחת יפת תאר
מאד וחסידה ונשאת שלשה פעמים לשלשה בני אדם ובכל לילה ראשון
של נשואיה למחרת מוצאים בעלה מת. אמרה לא ימותו עוד בני אדם
5 עלי אשב אלמנה ועגונה עד אשר יראה המקום וירחם. ישבה ימים
רבים והיה לאותו עשיר אח עני מאד במדינה אחרת והיו לו עשרה
בנים ובכל יום ויום הוא ובנו הגדול מביאין חבילי עצים מן היער
ומוכרין אותן ומזה היו מתפרנסים הוא ואשתו ובניו פעם אחת לא
מכרו ולא היה להם מעות לקנות לחם. ולא אכלו אותו היום. למחר
10 היה להם הלכו ביער ונתעטף רוח האב זלגו עיני הבן דמעות על עניים
ותלה עיניו למרום הרהר הבן בלבו ונטל רשות מאביו ומאמו והלך
למדינת דודו וכשבא לביתו שמח שמחה גדולה דודו עליו וגם אשתו
ובתו ושאלו לו על אביו ועל אמו ועל הבני' ישב עמו שבעה ימים לסוף
שבעה ימים בא הבחור לדודו אמר לו שאלה אחת אני שואל ממך
15 אל תשיבני. אמר לו דודו אמור בני מה שתרצה אמר לו השבעה לי וכן
עשה. אמר זאת השאלה אשר אני שואל ממך שתתן לי בתך לאשה.
כששמע האיש כבה אמר לו אל בני אל כי בעונותי כך מדתה. אמר
לו על מנת כך. אמר לו אם על עסקי ממוני אתה קופץ עליה אל

תשאנה ואני אתן לך כסף וזהב הרבה כי אתה בחור נאה וחכם
ובעצתי אל תמתכן בה. אמר לו כבר נשבעת על הדבר הזה ראה
העשיר הדבר ונתרצה לו ובא לבתו וספר לה את הדברים כששמעה
זאת בכתה וצעקה במר נפשה ותלתה עיניה למרום ואמרה רבון העולמים
תהי ידך בי ואל ימותו כל אלו עלי. מה עשה קדשה ועשה משתה וקרא 5
לזקני העיר ועשה כילה וישב החתן בתוכה ונזדמן לו זקן אחד והוא אליהו
ז״ל וקראו בינו לבינו ואמר לו בני איעצך עצה נכונה ואל תמ מעצתי.
כשתשב לסעוד יבא עליך עני לבוש בגדים שחורים וקרועים יחף וינע
שער נתנו מסמרים עני שאין כמוהו בכל העולם כשתראהו תקום ממושבך
ותושיבהו אצלך והאכילהו והשקהו ושמש לפניו בכל כהן וכבדהו ואל 10
תפל דבר מכל אשר דברתי לך ותשאר לשלום ואני אלך לדרכי. הלך
לו הזקן ובא החתן למקומו ישבו על המשתה כשהתחילו לאכל בא אותו
עני וכשראהו החתן עמד ממקומו ועשה לו כל מה שאמר לו הזקן.
לאחר המשתה אותו העני קרא לחתן הביאו לחדר אמר לו בני אני
שלוחו של מקום ובאתי הנה לקחת את נפשך, אמר לו אדני תן לי זמן 15
שנה אחת או חצי שנה א״ל לא אעשה. אמר לו אם כן תן לי שלשים
יום או שבעה ימי המשתה אמר לו לא אתן לך אפילו יום אחד כי
כבר הגיע עתך. אמר לו בבקשה ממך המתן לי עד שאלך ואקח רשות
מאשתי אמר לו לדבר הזה אשא פניך ולך ובא מהרה הלך לחדר והיא
יושבת יחידה ובוכה ומתפללת לקונה ופתח החדר קרא הבחור אליה 20
ובאת לפתוח לו הביאתו אצלה בחדר החזיקה בו ונשקה לו. אמרה
לו אחי למה באת אמר לה ליטול רשות ממך כי בא עתי ללכת כדרך
כל הארץ כי המלאך בא והגיד לי שבא לבקש את נפשי. אמרה לו לא
תלך אלא חשב הנה ואני אלך לו ואדברה עמו הלכה ומצאה אותו
אמרה לו אתה המלאך שבאת לבקש נפש אישי אמר לה הן. אמרה 25
לו לא ימות עתה כתוב בתורה כי יקח איש אשה חדשה לא יצא בצבא

ולא יעבור עליו לכל דבר נקי יהיה לביתו שנה אחת ושמח את אשתו אשר
לקח והק"בה אמת ותורתו אמת. ואם תקח את נפשו תעשה התורה
פלסתר אם תקבל דברי מוטב ואם לאו תבא עמי לבי' דין הגדול לפני
הק"בה מיד גער הב"ה במלאך והלך לו. בלילה שכבו יחד החתן והכלה.
5 ואבי הכלה ואמה בוכים בחדרם וכשהגיע לחצי הלילה קמו האיש
והאשה להכין קבר לחתנם קודם שיעלה עמוד השחר. כשקמו שמעו
החתן והכלה משחקין ושמחים יחד נכנסו לחדר לראות הדבר ראו
ושמחו והודיעו הדבר לקהל והודו לשם. וזהו שהק"בה נוצר
הבוטחים בו :

APPENDIX.

A. BEL AND THE DRAGON.

מדרש רבה דרבה פרשת וישב יעקב בפסוק וישליכו אותו
הבורה: קראתי בשמך י׳ מבור תחתיות °זה דניאל שנתפלל לפני
הקֹבֹה מן הבור ושמע הקֹבֹה קול תפלתו והצילו מן האריות ההֹד קולֹי
שמעת גׁ קרבת ביום אקראך גׁ וכן הוא או אלהי שלח מלאכיה וסגר
פום אריוותא ולא חבלוני כל קבל די קדמוהי זכו השתכחת לי. ולא   5
די שהצילו אלא שנקמו מאויביו ההֹד י׳ ריבי נפשי גאלת חיי וכן הוא
אומׁ ואמר מלכא והתיו גובריא אליך די אכלו קורצוהי די דניאל
ולגוב אריוותא רמו אינן בניהון ונשיהון ולא מטו לארעית גובא עד
די שליטו בהון אריוותא וכל גרמיהון הדיקו. הרי מצינו שניצל דניאל
מן הבור מן המקרא ורבותינו אמרו מסורת היא בידינו שפעם אחרת   10
ניצל דניאל מבור אריות בימי כרש הפרסי על שכפר בעֹז וביערה
אמרו :

מלכא אסטיגוס[1] אתאסף על אבהתיה וקביל כורש פרסאה מלכותיה
ודניאל איתווא איקרייה עם דמלכא ועמד ווא עם מלכא ומשבח
ווא מן כולהון וחמוי דמלכא ואיתווא פתכרא חד לבבלי דשמיה ביל   15
ומפקין ווא עלוי נפקתא כל יום סמידא תרי עשר ארדבין ודיכרי
ארבעין וחמרא שית מתרין והוה מֹלכא דחיל ווא ליה ואזיל ווא ליה

הוא דריוש המדי .Marg [1]

כל יום וסגיד ווא ליה ודניאל סגיד ווא לאלהא. ואמר מלכא לדניאל
מטול מאן לא סגדת לבל אלהי. אמר ליה דניאל לא סגידנא לצלמא
ולפתכרא ולגליפא מטול דעובד אידיא דבני אינשא הוא אלא אנא
דחילנא לאלהא חייא הוא דעבד שמיא וארעא ואיתוי מרא על כל
5 בשר ליה סגידנא. ואמר מלכא לדניאל לא מיתחזי לך דביל חי הוא
או לא חזית דהא אכיל ושתי כל יום הידין דניאל גחך ואמר למלכא
לא תיטעי מלכא *דהכא מן לגיו דטינא יד[1] ומן לבר דנחשא ומידם
מן זומוי לא אכל ולא אישתי. הידין איתחמית מלכא וקרא לכומרוי
דביל ואמר להון אי לא תימרון לי דמאן אכיל נפקתא הדא כולה
10 תמותון ואין תחוונן לי דביל אכיל נימות דניאל דגדיף על ביל. אמר
דניאל ניהוי אך מילתך מלכא והויין ווא כומרוי דביל שבעין סטר מן
נשיהון ובניהון. ואתא מלכא הוא ודניאל לביתיה דביל ואמרין כומריא
למלכא הא חנן נפקינן לן לבר והת[2] מלכא שים מכולתא לביל ומזוג
חמרא וסים ואחוד תרעא וחתים בעיזקתך וקדים ותא בצפרא אין לא
15 תשכח אינון לכולהון מיכלאתא דאכל אינון ביל נימות אנן ואין הוא
דאכל אינון ביל נימות דניאל היז[3] דגדיף עלינון. והינון מטול דתכילי
ווא דעביד ווא להון מעלנא בטיישא תחות פתורא וביה עלין ווא
ונקפין ואכלן כל מידם דמתסימווא ליה לביל ושקלין מידם דייתר.
כד [דין] נפקו כומריה דביל אייתי מלכא מיכלאתא ומלא פתורא
20 וסם קדם ביל ומלא חמרא מאניה אך עייאדהון ונפק ואמר דניאל
לטלי ווא אייתון לי קיטמא וערב ליה בערבילא קדמוי דמלכא בכוליה
ביתיה דביל וחזא מלכא ונפק ואחד תרעא וחתמיה מלכא בעזקתיה
ובעזקת דניאל וכומרי אזלי בליליא אך דמעאדין ווא הינון ונשיהון
ובניהון ואכלו כל מידם דמתסמווא לביל ואשתיו חמרא. וקדים מלכא

[1] Plg. הו. [2] So. Plg. אית. [3] Plg. הו. הנא גר מן לגו דטינא הו

בצפרא ודניאל עמיה ואזלו לתמן ואמר מלכא לדניאל קיימין חתמי

דניאל אמר דניאל קיימין מר מלכא והוה דכד פתח תרעא אדיק מלכא

על פתורא וחזא דאיכיל ווא כל מידם דאיתסים לביל ויהב קלא רמא

על תרעא מן לבר ואמר את ביל ולית לוותך מיכלא אוף לא קליל

הידין דניאל גחך ולבביה¹ דמלכא דלא ניעול לגיו עד שעתא ואמר 5

דניאל למלכא חור מר מלכא ואתבקא בארעא עיקבאתא הינן דמאן

איתינן ואמר מלכא חזינא עיקבאתא בארעא דגברי ודנשי ודטליי.

הידין איתחמית מלכא ולבך² אינון לכומרי ולנשיהון ולבניהון וחוינון

למלכא מעלנא דאיתווא להון בטישא היו³ דביה עליק⁴ ווא ונפקין

ואכלין כל מידם דמיתסימווא ליה לביל על פתורא וקטלינן מלכא 10

לכולהון ולביל יהביה מיהבתא לדניאל ותבריה דניאל וסחף היכליה:

◊ נשלם מעשה ביל צלם הכשדים ◊

❖ עניָן מיטול תנינא הוא הנקרא משא התנין ❖

איתווא תוף תמן תנינא רבא דסגדין ליה בבלאי. ואמר מלכא

לדניאל הנונא⁵ על הנא לא משבחת דתימר עלוי דליו אלהא ווא סגיד

ליה מטול דאלהא ווא חייא. אמר דניאל למלכא אנא לוי׳ אלהי

סגידנא מטול דהנו אלהא חייא ואת מלכא הב לי עלוי שולטנא ואנא 15

קטילנא ליה לתנינא הנא דלא סייפא ודלא חוטרא ואמר מלכא יהיב

לך. ונסב דניאל זיפתא וסערא ותרבא ובשלינון אך חדא ועבד מנהון

אספירי ואישרי אינון בפומיה דתנינא ואתבזע ומית ואמר דניאל הא

חזו דחלתכון בבלאי. והוה דכד שמעו בבלאי אתבאש להון סגי⁶

¹ Plg. ואחדה.   ² Plg. ואחד.   ³ Plg. הו.   ⁴ Plg. עלין.
⁵ Plg. השא.   ⁶ See Pugio Fidei, p. 742.

ואתכנשון על מלכא ואתהפיכו עלוי ואמרין חד לחד יהודאה הוה ליה
למלכא לביל תבר ולתנינא קטל ולכומרי קטלינן ואיתון גב מלכא
אמרין ליה או אשלם לן לדניאל ואי לא קטלינן לך ולביתך. חזא
מלכא דקמו עלוי כלהון אכחדא ואתאלץ ליה ואלצאית אשלמיה להון
5 לדניאל והינון דברינון לדניאל *ואזל גבינוי¹ בגובא דאריוואתא והוה
חמן אשתא יומין וחפונוי באבנא וחתמונוי בעזקתא דמלכא ובגושפנקהון
והוה חמן אישתא יומין אך דניכפינון אריוואתא וניכלונוי ואיתוא ביה
בגובא היו אריוואתא שבעה ויהבין ווא להון תרין פגרין ביומא ותרין
(דוכרין) דכרין ובהנין יומאתא לא יהבו להון מידם דניכלון אך
10 דניכפינון ונאכלונוי לדניאל. ואיתווא חבקוק נביאה ביהוד בשיל בישולא
ופת פתי בערבא וארמי ביה ואזל דנוביל לחקלא לחצדיה. ואמר ליה
מלאכיה דיי׳ זיל אוביל מיוכלתא הדא די עלך לדניאל דרמי בגוב
אריוואתא בבבל. אמר חבקוק מר לא חזיא לי בבל ולגובא לא ידענא
ליה. ואשדי מלאכא אידיה על רישיה דחבקוק ושקליה בסערא דרישיה
15 וסאמיה לבבל לעיל מן גובא בעותא דרוחא דקודשא וקרא חבקוק
ואמר דניאל דניאל קום שקול שירותא הדא דשדר לך אלהא אמר
דניאל אתדכרן אלהא ולא שבק רחמוי מיני וידענא דלא שבקת
לאיילין דרחמין לך וקם דניאל ואכל ושקליה מלאכא לחבקוק ביה
בשעתא ואקימיה באתרא דשקליה הייך דהוו מן קדם דין. ואתא מלכא
20 ליומא דשבעה למיבכי על דניאל מטול דבריאות ליה עלוי ואתא לות
גובא ואדיק בגובא וחזייה לדניאל כד יתיב ויהב קלא רמא ואמר רב
הוא אלהיה דדניאל ואסקיה לדניאל מן גובא ולבעיל דבבוי² דדניאל
הינין דאכלו קורצוי ובעון למיקטליה אשדי אינון בגובא ובה בשעתא
אכלו אינון אריוואתא קדמוי דמלכא וקדם דניאל:

---

¹ ואזל כאמוניו (סאמוניו?); Pugio Fidei (סאמוניו) ואזלי ארמיוהי Plg.

² ולבעלי דבבוי Pugio Fidei.

לכך נאמר צמתו בבור חיי ודו אבן בי צפו מים על ראשי
אמרתי נגזרתי קראתי שמך יי' מבור תחתיות: נמצא ששני
פעמים הושלך דניאל לבור אחד בימי דריוש המדי ואחד בימי
כורש הפרסי חתנו ובראשונה לא עמד בו אלא לילה אחת וניצל
ובשניה עמד בו שבעה ימים וניצל וזה המעשה השני לא נכתב 5
בספרי הקדש נראה כי לפי שהיה הצדיק מלומד בנם זה דיו להזכר
פעם אחת:

שני המעשים האלו ר"ל מעשה ביל צלם הכשדים ומשא התנין
כללום הנצרים בכלל עשרים וארבעה ספרי הנביאים עם
שלשה ספרים אחרים ואמר המעתיק שלהם   10
כי לא מצאם בלשון הקדש:

B. EXTRACT FROM THE B'RESHITH RABBAH,
§ 68.

דבר אחר והנה ה' נצב עליו. והנה מלאכי אלהים זה דניאל עולים
ויורדים בו שעלה והוצא את בלעו מתוך פיו הה"ד ופקדתי על בל
בבבל והוצאתי את בלעו מפיו שהיה לו תנין אחד לנבוכדנצר והיה
בולע כל מה שהיו משליכין לפניו אמר ליה נבוכדנצר לדניאל במה 15
כוחו גדול שבולע כל מה שמשליכין לפניו אמר לו דניאל תן לי רשות
ואני מתישו נתן לו רשות מה עשה נטל תבן והטמין לתוכו מסמרים
השליך לפניו ונקבו מסמרים את בני מעיו הדא הוא דכתיב הוצאתי את
בילעו מפיו: